CIVIC
BUILDINGS
AFTER
THE
SPANISH-
AMERICAN
WAR

CARIBBEAN
STUDIES
SERIES

Anton L. Allahar and Natasha Barnes
Series Editors

CIVIC BUILDINGS AFTER THE SPANISH-AMERICAN WAR

MARIA EUGENIA ACHURRA G.

UNIVERSITY PRESS OF MISSISSIPPI / JACKSON

The University Press of Mississippi is the scholarly publishing agency of
the Mississippi Institutions of Higher Learning: Alcorn State University,
Delta State University, Jackson State University, Mississippi State University,
Mississippi University for Women, Mississippi Valley State University,
University of Mississippi, and University of Southern Mississippi.

www.upress.state.ms.us

The University Press of Mississippi is a member
of the Association of University Presses.

Library of Congress Cataloging-in-Publication Data

Names: Achurra G., Maria Eugenia, author.
Title: Civic buildings after the Spanish-American War / Maria Eugenia
Achurra G.
Other titles: Caribbean studies series.
Description: Jackson : University Press of Mississippi, 2023. | Series:
Caribbean studies series | Includes bibliographical references and
index.
Identifiers: LCCN 2023037663 (print) | LCCN 2023037664 (ebook) | ISBN
9781496847577 (hardback) | ISBN 9781496847584 (trade paperback) | ISBN
9781496847591 (epub) | ISBN 9781496847607 (epub) | ISBN 9781496847614
(pdf) | ISBN 9781496847621 (pdf)
Subjects: LCSH: Public architecture—United States. | Public
architecture—Latin America. | Eclecticism in architecture—United
States. | Eclecticism in architecture—Latin America. |
Architecture—United States—History—19th century. |
Architecture—United States—History—20th century. |
Architecture—Latin America—History.
Classification: LCC NA9050.5 .A248 2023 (print) | LCC NA9050.5 (ebook) |
DDC 720.973/0904—dc23/eng/20230925
LC record available at https://lccn.loc.gov/2023037663
LC ebook record available at https://lccn.loc.gov/2023037664

British Library Cataloging-in-Publication Data available

CONTENTS

ACKNOWLEDGMENTS

For the completion of this book, much gratitude is owed to Raquel Talbott, Protocol Office of the Organization of American States, Washington, DC; Brandi Oswald, archivist, Cartographic Branch, National Archives and Records Administration, College Park, Maryland; Geography and Map Division, Library of Congress; Prints and Photographs Division, Library of Congress; Jason L. Hoffmann, Bayh/Indiana Field Office, and Daniel A. Wang, property manager, Frank E. Moss Courthouse, General Services Administration; Jennifer Parker and Viveca Robichaud, University of Notre Dame Architecture Library; Professor Julio César Pérez Hernández, University of Notre Dame School of Architecture; Dr. Laurie Ortíz Rivera and Elena García Orozco, Architecture Library, University of Puerto Rico, Precinct of Río Piedras; Paul Philippe Cret Collection, Architectural Archives, University of Pennsylvania; Allison Olsen, Architectural Archives, University of Pennsylvania; Philadelphia Architects and Buildings Project; Elaine Straka, Interlibrary Loan Department, Cleveland Public Library; Melanie Rapp-Weiss, Brecksville Branch, Cuyahoga County Public Library; Autry Museum, Los Angeles; Collection of the US House of Representatives; Chicago History Museum; Rowman and Littlefield; Ryerson and Burnham Art and Architecture Archives, Art Institute of Chicago; British Library; George A. Smathers Libraries, University of Florida; Google Earth; USDA/National Agricultural Library; Granger Historical Picture Archive; Newberry Library; Special Collections, University of Texas at Arlington Libraries; Archives of American Art, Smithsonian Institution; Archives of American Gardens, Smithsonian Institution; San Diego Historical Society; Frederick Law Olmsted National Historical Site; New-York Historical Society; John K. Turpin and W. Barry Thomson; José Chez Checo; Andrés Mignucci; Lorenz & Williams, Dayton, Ohio; Jennifer Krivickas and Elizabeth Meyer, the Robert A. Deshon & Karl J. Schlachter Library for Design, Architecture, Art, and Planning,

University of Cincinnati; and the Interlibrary Loan Department, University of Cincinnati Libraries.

My deepest gratitude goes to Dr. Patrick Snadon, Dr. Edson Cabalfin, and particularly Dr. Jeffrey Tilman, to whom I owe the completion of my book. Also, I extend my deepest gratitude to Dr. Rebecca Williamson at the University of Cincinnati School of Architecture and Interior Design for her support.

I also dedicate this work to Basilia González and Joseph Turocy, for their encouragement and commitment to this just cause.

To all, thank you.

CIVIC
BUILDINGS
AFTER
THE
SPANISH-
AMERICAN
WAR

INTRODUCTION

At the dawn of the twentieth century, the United States strengthened its geopolitical grip on territories acquired after the 1898 Spanish-American War, either permanently or temporarily—first Cuba and Puerto Rico, then Panama and the Dominican Republic. With its nationalistic presence on foreign land, the US government influenced magnificent examples of civic architecture, regularly erecting them independently of the local jurisdiction and consequently investing its possessions with the excellence and grandeur of the Beaux-Arts tradition.

Overseas, audiences adopted such stylistic canons as restraint, harmony, symmetry, and order. By mapping their exuberant sceneries, selected landmarks allured viewers via vantage points through grand avenues flanked by woodland or human-made amenities. From elevated locations, spectators summoned up their palatine spirit.

Why would the United States endorse this kind of aesthetics? To consolidate and perpetuate the American Dream. These urban installations and formal premises still portray the power and grandeur of Progressive America. As imperialist backdrops, these buildings still convey majesty and distinction to their visitors. Standing tall as guardians of a bygone era, they still engage Americans and others who enjoy digging into the exceptionalist past.

What is territory or possession? It is a region or site where a dominating regime manipulates indigenous people's traditional beliefs and languages, culture and ways of thought, art, architecture, and infrastructure, demonstrating the regime's firm hold.

Despite the magnificence of these works, US aspirations ran deeper. It exerted a firm control over the war and its repercussions, snatching key locations across the board and covering them under its nationalistic umbrella.

"Goff's Historical Map of the Spanish-American War in the West Indies, 1898" (Chicago: Fort Dearborn Publishing, 1899). Courtesy of the Geography and Map Division, Library of Congress.

CEAN

GULF
OF
MEXICO

MORRO CASTLE
CABANA CASTLE
Batteries
San Diego Fort
Morro Light
LA PUNTA CASTLE
Casa Blanca
Prison
Batteries
Santa Clara Battery
Reina Battery
Cabana Barracks
Plaza de Armas
San Lazaro Hospital
Battery Military Headquarters
HAVANA
Cemetery
Hospital
Custom House Post Office
Tacon Theater
San Nazario Battery
Barracks de Belen
Principe Barracks
Cavalry Barracks
Artillery Barracks
HARBOR
PRINCIPE CASTLE
Depot
Military Hospital
ARSENAL AND NAVY YARD
Batteries
H A V A

U.S. battleship Maine, Capt. Sigsbee blown up Feb. 15, 1898. 260 lives lost.

Military Storehouse
Battery and Magazine
Station
ATARES CASTLE

HAVANA
CITY AND HARBOR.

Powder Magazine

DOMINGO I.

TO DOMINGO

ST. DOMINGO

Fort and batteries bombarded by Adl. May 12
Naval station off harbor St. Paul and Terror, June 22.
Light house seized, Aug. 1.

SAN JUAN

MONA PASSAGE

VIRGIN IS.

MAYAGUEZ
PUERTO RICO
Charlotte Amalie
St. Thomas

LEEWARD IS.

PONCE
GUAYAMA

LESSER

Occupied by Americans, Aug. 11.

ANTILLES

St. Kitts

St. Johns

Guadeloupe

Basse Terre

Dominica

Martinique
Fort de France

St. Lucia

WINDWARD IS.

St. Vincent

Kingstown
The Grenadines
Barbados
Bridgetown

St. Georges
Grenada

GOFF'S HISTORICAL MAP OF THE
NISH-AMERICAN WAR
IN THE
EST INDIES, 1898

Copyrighted, 1899, by Eugenia Wheeler Goff, and Henry Slade Goff, authors of
Goff's Historical Maps for Schools and Families.

FORT DEARBORN PUB. CO.
MAP ENGRAVERS AND PUBLISHERS
CHICAGO, ILL.

Cuba 129

West Indies
G28-1898-6336
Compliments of the Authors

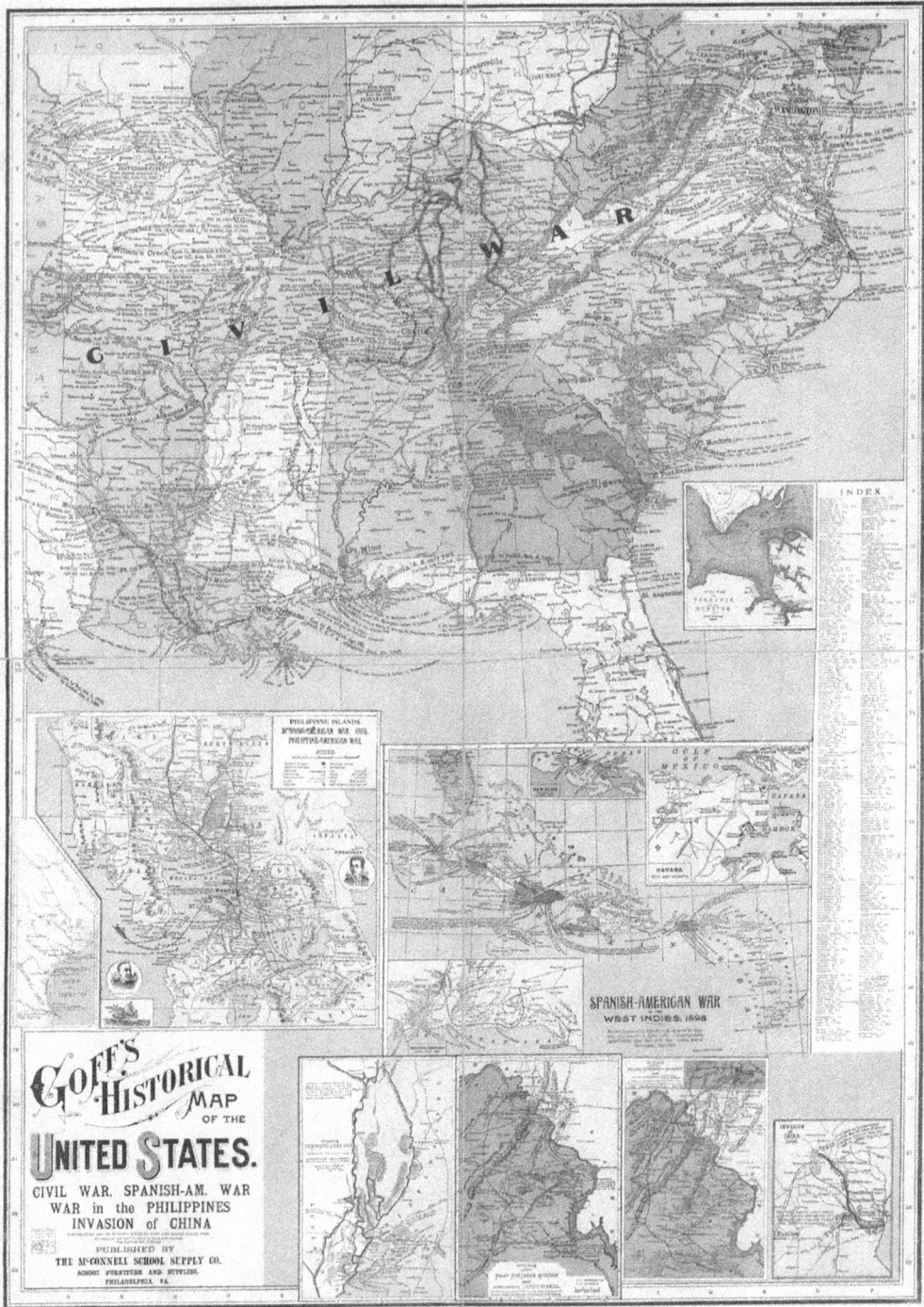

"Goff's Historical Map of the United States Civil War, Spanish-Am. War, War in the Philippines, Invasion of China" (Philadelphia: McConnell School Supply, 1907). Courtesy of the Geography and Map Division, Library of Congress.

Foreign populations faced an existential dilemma: after being considered the Other, how could they associate such dystopian dreams of grandeur with a territorial ethos?

More than a century after the end of the Spanish-American War and the beginning of World War I (1914–18), Puerto Rico's Capitolio (Capitol Building) (1929), the Cuba's Capitolio (National Capitol) (1929), and the Dominican Republic's Palacio Nacional (National Palace) keep their doors open to visitors. The Panama Canal Administration Building (1914) concealed its civic functions in the former Canal Zone with a subdued, "hidden" dome. Its worldwide mercantile and strategic operations demanded a more austere, semi-astylar appearance.

This book highlights these unique scenarios. It starts by defining exceptionalism and its role in government US Beaux-Arts federal architecture. It then delves into Beaux-Arts civic architecture in the continental United States and Latin America. Finally, it describes the works of relevant designers of these facilities and their urban layouts.

In so doing, this book reflects on the expansionist spirit of US government architecture as evidenced in construction on foreign soil. The magnificent amenities of overseas architecture in the decades after the Spanish-American War still capture the ethos of Progressive America.

CHAPTER 1

AMERICAN EXCEPTIONALISM
Artistic and Architectural Precedents

An Exceptionalist Spectacle

"Uncle Sam digging under the influence of the Sons of Ohio at the right place." So ran a toast proposed at the twenty-second annual banquet of the Cincinnati Commercial Club at the Queen City Club on November 13, 1902. The reference was to the role Ohioans had played in the decision of the United States to construct an interoceanic canal in Panama, and the man who offered the toast was in a position to know whereof he spoke. He was Philippe Bunau-Varilla, a French engineer who had served the De Lesseps enterprise in Panama in the 1880's and, when the French venture failed, had kept faith with the project and eventually turned to the United States to rescue it. His speech-making and lobbying activities in the United States in 1901 and 1902 were legend. And from that night he would go on to participate in the Panama revolution of 1903, become Panama's first minister to the United States, and negotiate the treaty under which the United States secured the right to construct the Panama Canal.
—Charles D. Ameringer, "Ohio and the Panama Canal"

Which formal and tectonic components (if any) are shared by civic buildings constructed after the Spanish-American War? Moreover, can they be regarded as vestiges of the Monroe Doctrine? As epitaphs for the set of beliefs that American journalist John O'Sullivan labeled Manifest Destiny in 1845?

In 1823, John Quincy Adams (1767–1848), secretary of state under US president James Monroe (1758–1831), issued what became known as the Monroe

Doctrine, a set of policies regarding the newly independent Latin American democracies. These nations had obtained freedom from the Spanish colonial system via civic and military movements led by such notable emancipators as the Liberator, Simón Bolívar (1783–1830), Bernardo O'Higgins (1778–1842), and José de San Martín (1778–1850). But the United States drew up the Monroe Doctrine without significant consultation with the young nations.

The Monroe Doctrine enjoined European countries from meddling in Latin America, thereby enforcing the US role as a paternalist watchdog in the Western Hemisphere. In the early 1880s, secretary of state James G. Blaine (1830–93), serving under US president James A. Garfield (1831–81), annexed to the doctrine a "Big Brother" policy to facilitate Latin American nations entering the US trade market. And in 1904, US president Theodore Roosevelt (1858–1919) attached a corollary that condoned US intervention in Latin American countries in case of any possible European intrusion. In this context, the Calvo Doctrine (1868) and the Drago Doctrine (1902) emerged as Latin American reactions to the Monroe Doctrine and the Roosevelt Corollary, trying to protect new democracies and their geopolitical and legal status from foreign interference. Instead of a manifesto or a set of rules, Manifest Destiny endorsed an implicit, Democratic predisposition toward appropriation that diverged from a more traditional dominance through law and faith.

The Monroe Doctrine and Manifest Destiny eventually led to the idea of American exceptionalism. In the United States, the concept of exceptionalism emulates Frederick Jackson Turner's essay *The Significance of the Frontier in American History* (1893). Although Turner never uses the term, he alludes to its economic and political conditions by defining a process of expansionism driven by a Germanic thirst for crossing a continent and winning a wilderness.[1] He compares the continental eastern mindset to that of the West, which he portrays as a frontier ready to be conquered. In Turner's view, as the United States had gained, acquired, or settled a new territory, the resulting process of multiculturalization (or Americanization) had generated US achievements and contributions.

Turner's essay constitutes an early predecessor of Julian Go's definition of exceptionalism, which includes both oppression and power.[2] Although the United States is a democracy, its expansionist spirit led it to snatch the Great Plains and the West from the Native Americans and to acquire foreign land, a process that was evident as early as 1803 with the Louisiana Purchase and that continued through the Mexican War in the mid-1840s.

Not all exceptionalisms hold the same connotations. Indeed, every contemporary definition of power rests on its intentionality. With regard to the potential for dominance in an exceptionalist scenery, the terms *acquisition*

John Gast, *American Progress* (1872). Courtesy of the Autry Museum, Los Angeles. 92.126.1.

and *implementation* differ in their logistics and tactics. In Go's formulation, exceptionalism becomes another version of Eurocentrism, but it is not exclusive to nations from the other side of the Atlantic. In general, each nationalistic scenario determines what makes other countries "exceptional," "unique," or "different," exalting their "flawless" past and "pristine" future. Strategic foreign soil becomes "an object of desire through such tantalizing denominators."[3]

Go compares the American and British governing patterns—their values, political institutions, and traditions. Rather than being "assimilative," American geopolitical models become "associative." However, while their beliefs and connotations had British roots, the corresponding architectural and stylistic forms were primarily French.

Did artistic trends such as landscape paintings from the Progressive Era play a relevant role in this geopolitical scenario? Were other disciplines also involved, such as land surveying? And if so, how did Manifest Destiny interact with them?

Art critics and historians have extensively discussed the impact of American exceptionalism in the arts beginning in the 1800s. In *The Magisterial Gaze: Manifest Destiny and American Landscape, c. 1830–1865* (1991), Albert Boime argues that both the Monroe Doctrine and Manifest Destiny permeated their audiences' proselytized ways of seeing. For him, pictorial compositions became representations that, akin to the invention of the photographic camera, helped Western-centered audiences acquire a visual taste for an American wilderness. This understanding is useful in interpreting the role of civic architecture between the American Civil War (1861–65) and World War II (1939–45). Through their new government constructions, US territories showcased their exceptionalist representations.

This phenomenon is unique neither to the United States nor to the late nineteenth and early twentieth centuries. Nationalistic designs and parameters existed worldwide even before the Greek and Roman empires. From Paris to New York; from Washington, DC, to Manila; from Rhode Island to San Juan; from Chicago to Balboa, Panama, public facilities could transmute their monumentality across the land and the water. Lawrence Vale clarifies the relationship between spatial arrangements and the authority that created them. On the one hand, through a nationalism of aspiration, people endorse their dreams for independence. On the other hand, a nationalism of consolidation allows people to bring together hopes and strive for sovereignty.[4]

Architecture granted a sense of entitlement to its audiences through a Cartesian understanding of the world in which reason and logic prevailed over emotion. Such a sense of grandeur helped the United States disseminate its aesthetic prowess on both the mainland and elsewhere—and to face allegations of authority and control by its rivals. This sense of possession was American exceptionalism: those colonized became dependent on a nonegalitarian, elitist distribution of wealth and labor.

American progress became unstoppable through its active presence in territories and occupied land. Republican presidents Theodore Roosevelt (in office 1901–9) and William Howard Taft (1857–1930; in office 1909–13) sought "to speak softly and carry a big stick," as Roosevelt famously said.[5] The era also included the presidency of Democrat Woodrow Wilson (1856–1924; in office 1913–21).

The Tarsney Act

Prior to the early 1850s, the construction of US government buildings was not centralized or standardized. The architectural profession was almost nonexistent, and most civil structures such as customhouses were erected by masons or skilled tradesmen. Stylistic homogeneity was achieved largely by following classical orders. In the second half of the nineteenth century, however, the United States experienced a boom in public architecture to meet the rapidly growing country's demand for new courthouses, post offices, statehouses,

John Charles Tarsney, n.d. Collection of the US House of Representatives.

customhouses, and hospitals as well as other facilities. To oversee the design and construction of these buildings, the US Department of the Treasury founded the Office of the Supervising Architect in 1852 and staffed it with a large crew of draftspersons and clerks.

The office's first years of operation coincided with the emergence of architecture as a regulated profession. However, architects working in the public sector were disadvantaged relative to their private counterparts. Architects who came from wealthy families could visit Europe, updating their knowledge and learning new design and construction methods, but most public servants lacked access to these opportunities.

The construction of the State, War, and Navy Building (1871–88) in Washington, DC, under supervising architect Alfred B. Mullett (1834–90) demonstrated the problem. Its fragmented use of architectural orders stacked on multiple levels and its French Second Empire influences attracted criticism, with the building derided as a "mighty granite pile." In the face of such attacks, Mullett took his own life, and questions arose about the future of the Office of the Supervising Architect.[6]

That debate led Congress to pass legislation to change the office's operations. Passed by Congress in July 1892 and signed into law on February 20, 1893, the Tarsney Act, named after its principal supporter, US representative John Charles Tarsney (1845–1920), allowed the private sector to design and construct public installations.

Cass Gilbert, Alexander Hamilton US Custom House, New York City, 1907. Photo by author.

Cass Gilbert, Alexander Hamilton US Custom House, New York City, 1907. Courtesy of the Prints and Photographs Division, Library of Congress. L-12481, C-6372.

The act authorized the secretary of the treasury

to obtain plans, drawings, and specifications for the erection of public buildings for the United States, authorized by Congress to be erected under the supervision and direction of the Secretary of the Treasury and the local supervision of the construction thereof by competition among architects under such conditions as he may prescribe, and to make payment for expenses and for the services of said architects whose plan may be selected out of the appropriations for the respective buildings: Provided, That not less than five architects shall be invited by the said Secretary to compete for the furnishing of such plans and specifications and the supervision of such construction: And provided further, That the general supervision of the work shall continue in the office of the Supervising Architect of the Treasury Department.[7]

The Tarsney Act strongly influenced the 1893 World's Columbian Exposition in Chicago and its cutting-edge showcases. The White City also had an aesthetic impact on the production of public buildings: in 1900, the Office of the Supervising Architect widely implemented City Beautiful and Beaux-Arts forms. Progressive America paid court to the Tarsney Act for two decades, enhancing governmental and public installations and developing a branded architectural image. Real estate interests also overlapped with the act and its benefits.

Soon after its ratification, however, abuses of the Tarsney Act became flagrant. Federal officials awarded projects to colleagues and acolytes, while architects openly handed out bribes to obtain design commissions.

The design and construction of the New York Custom House triggered a major scandal involving architect Cass Gilbert (1859–1934) and supervising architect James Knox Taylor (1857–1929). Gilbert and Taylor had been business partners, and Gilbert had used his political leverage to help Taylor obtain his public position. Similar issues led to the repeal of the Tarsney Act in 1913.[8]

The City Beautiful Movement

In this context, how can Progressive architecture be interpreted as an "archaeology of a recent past"? After all, human dwellings become concrete strata for their adopted canons, building patterns, and spatial arrangements. Here, architectural history summons up permanent structures as "witnesses of foregone eras." Its environmental, technological, and historical parameters reveal how people have lived and constructed in defined settings.[9]

World's Columbian Exposition, Chicago, 1893. Courtesy of the Chicago History Museum. ICHi-025057.

The City Beautiful movement provided a historical catalyst. Its precedents date back to German philosopher Arthur Schopenhauer (1788–1860) and his influential work, *The World as Will and Representation* (1818–19). Schopenhauer delved into the human quest for "a more soothing, tranquil state of mind" to make spectators' experiences more pleasing.[10] He defined the arts through degrees of ethereal beauty. Since architecture steadily gravitated around matter and force, it remained at the base of an artistic, aesthetic pyramid that holds music at its apex. In addition, Cartesian knowledge served as a preamble to Schopenhauer's concept of the will. Advocates followed his philosophy of free will as a sort of determinism with illusionary freedom.

Schopenhauer's concept of beauty posited a binary dualism between detached connoisseurs and the public eye. An overwhelming, majestic sense of reverence, or quasi-fear, promoted a collective endorsement of experts such as architects, engineers, real estate agents, and government agencies. Most audiences lacked such knowledge. They leaned toward a world of appearance ruled by an elitist culture of aesthetic taste.

At the time, the American nation emulated the wealth and grandeur of its aristocracy, pursuing a beauty that returned to the Greek and Roman empires and their search for perfection. Architectural works from this era concurred with those earlier ideas, introducing spectators to classicist fashions, new gadgets, and technical accomplishments.

Reciprocally, the City Beautiful movement generated glamorous exhibits, state-of-the-art installations, and awe-inspiring world's fairs. Following London's Great Exhibition of 1851 and the Paris expositions of 1878, 1889, and 1900, giant world's fairs made spectators dream of new possibilities beyond reality. Audiences savored this aesthetic prowess by drifting aimlessly through the fairs' grand avenues, galleries, botanical gardens, and monuments.

As an urban design movement, City Beautiful opposed the "ugliness" and "vulgarity" of congested American metropolises. Such journalist-reformers as Ida Tarbell, Henry Demarest Lloyd, and Lincoln Steffens became outraged after witnessing the pernicious deterioration of US inner cities. Inspired by the English Garden City movement, City Beautiful amenities and urban layouts promoted such physical attributes as calculated rhythm and balanced proportions alongside the enhancement of workplaces and the fight against illness and vermin. Cleanness, whiteness, neatness, polished surfaces, proper ventilation, and lighting of interiors and exteriors became clear cultural and social measures of progress.

The World's Columbian Exposition adopted City Beautiful as its baseline. Daniel Hudson Burnham (1846–1912) coordinated the design and construction of pavilions with renowned architects Charles Follen McKim (1847–1909), Richard Morris Hunt (1827–1895; the first American to graduate from the École des Beaux-Arts), and Louis Henry Sullivan (1856–1924), among others. Following the principles of the Beaux-Arts, the idea was to create grand federal monuments to progress. By adopting classical forms and proportions, architects showed an image of a beautiful city, a city that would integrate tradition and innovation, a city of which all Americans—even the underprivileged—would dream.

In her 1893 poem "America the Beautiful," Katharine Lee Bates directly referred to the World's Fair by calling up visions of "alabaster cities":

> O beautiful for patriot dream
> That sees beyond the years
> Thine alabaster cities gleam
> Undimmed by human tears!
> America! America!

God shed His grace on thee
And crown thy good with brotherhood
From sea to shining sea![11]

Visual ostentation became a significant feature of the White City with its Beaux-Arts pavilions and monuments. With the exception of Sullivan's Transportation Building, which used gold and earthy hues, all of the buildings were painted white, creating a sense of uniformity. Most government architecture soon came to emulate the City Beautiful identity. To some extent, the fair supported an era of aesthetic cleansing or formal eugenics, in architecture, an orientation that Paul Cret reiterated in the 1920s and 1930s for his modern stripped classicism.

Other world's fairs, such as the 1901 Pan-American Exposition in Buffalo, New York, and the 1902 Colonial and International Exposition in New York City, as well as pavilions from the Louisiana Purchase Exposition (also known as the St. Louis World's Fair), also influenced civic works. In St. Louis, Isaac S. Taylor (1850–1917), who headed the fair's Commission of Architects, retained such architects as Gilbert, Burnham, Eames & Young, and Carrère and Hastings.

Taylor selected a French-born architect, Emmanuel Louis Masqueray (1861–1917), as chief of design. Masqueray had previously worked with John Mervin Carrère (1858–1911) and Thomas Hastings (1860–1929) and had studied with them at the École des Beaux-Arts. Taylor also selected George Edward Kessler (1862–1923) to prepare the site layout. Kessler, a German American city planner and landscape architect, was also an original member of the US Commission of Fine Arts and an acolyte of Frederick Law Olmsted (1822–1903).

Through a myriad of pavilions arranged along grand avenues, breathtaking parks, and majestic artificial lakes, world's fairs showcased "new," "exotic," and "outstanding" installations. Such exhibits epitomized a nationalistic age of architectural aesthetics. Their works glorified new American territories and occupied land via the construction of ephemeral and quasi-celestial white cities.

The City Beautiful movement summoned collective responsiveness to design new public amenities that could uplift the American spirit. Only progress could then awaken such attitudes among its audiences.

The École des Beaux-Arts and the Architecture of the Tarsney Act Era

Instruction at the École des Beaux-Arts was rational, rigid, and strenuous. Admission was restricted to men between fifteen and thirty years old who demonstrated the solid artistic and technical foundations that would enable them to endure four years of training. In contrast with the *École Polytechnique* (which introduced engineers to the architectural tradition), training at the École des Beaux-Arts introduced *concours* (competitions) and *rendus* (breathtaking large-scale renderings). Students could compete for the coveted Grand Prix in their last year, entitling winners to study at the French Academy in Rome.

Design standards at the École were eminently classical, going back to the ancient legacies of the Greeks and Romans and stressed rationalism as well as classical design orders and canons. The rational influences of Étienne-Louis Boullée (1728–99) and Claude-Nicolas Ledoux (1736–1806) became widely accepted. Moreover, architectural treatises such as Vitruvius's *Ten Books on Architecture*, John Ruskin's *Seven Lamps of Architecture* (1849), and Eugène Viollet-le-Duc's *Dictionnaire raisonné de l'architecture française du XIe au XVIe siècle* (1858–68) played significant roles in the instruction of young American architects.

Abbé Marc-Antoine Laugier's (1713–69) *Essay on Architecture* (1753) also endorsed such academic standards. Laugier traced the origins of architecture back to primitive huts, defining branches and limbs as precedents for traditional construction elements such as columns, beams, and rafters. Enclosures could return to their basics amid socioeconomic, geopolitical, and historical turmoil. In other words, in addition to classical orders and Euclidean shapes, precincts could always turn to nature for validating compositional and structural principles.

In contrast to the general academic and design principles of the Beaux-Arts, the Néo-Grecs emerged as an extreme, eccentric strain from the traditional instruction at the École. While Italian and French Renaissance influences regulated the curriculum, Mannerist and Baroque allusions implicitly became aberrations. In *The Architecture of the École des Beaux-Arts*, Neil Levine depicts French Néo-Grec architect Henri Labrouste (1801–75) as miscast at the École.

Labrouste was a strict follower of classical architecture and one of the École's most experienced instructors. His students' designs incorporated iron-frame construction and a more relaxed interpretation of the classical orders. He is widely known for his Bibliothèque Sainte-Geneviève (1838–50) in Paris. His legacy surpassed French frontiers, influencing many buildings abroad, including McKim, Mead & White's Boston Public Library at Copley Square (1895). Labrouste became one of the precursors of the modern movement in architecture. He also faced the scorn of his colleagues. Labrouste's students never won any major competitions at the École, and most struggled to receive their diplomas.

Most École alumni, however, remained primarily concerned with adhering to its founding design principles. The American Academy in Rome, founded

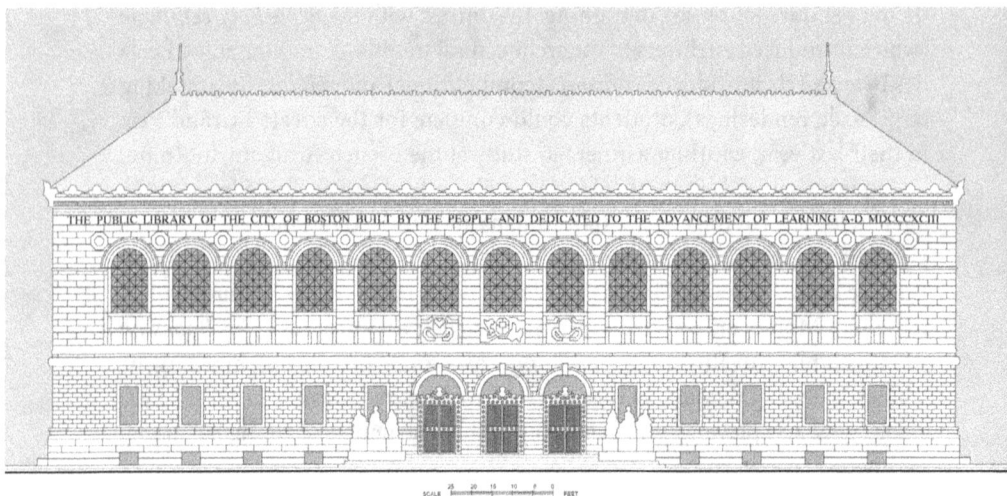

Charles Follen McKim, Boston Public Library, 1895. AutoCAD elevation by author from existing 1893 drawing.
Courtesy of Rowman & Littlefield.

in 1893 by McKim, a graduate of the École, strictly followed classical canons, with no tolerance for early modern architecture. McKim became committed to creating opportunities for young American architects to learn how to make "good" designs abroad, and the academy became an acceptable alternative to the rigid, austere École.

At the dawn of the twentieth century, the École and its alumni were forced to accept progress as a reality, but they did so slowly and cautiously. Such thinking raises a few questions. How does the influence of the École des Beaux-Arts relate to Progressive civil works? And within such an ostracizing educational system, why did the US government advocate an unabridged endorsement of the École's design alternatives to create public buildings on the mainland and abroad?

In *The Civic Architecture of Paul Cret*, Elizabeth Greenwell Grossman highlights two Beaux-Arts design patterns from the Progressive Era.[12] One of them, exemplified by McKim, Mead & White's Boston Public Library, reciprocally evoked elegance and restraint. The building was conceived from the outside, creating an American classicist style with perplexing functional solutions. A second pattern, represented by Carrère & Hastings and Paul Philippe Cret (1876–1945), kept fewer ties to a rigid Beaux-Arts or Modern French tradition. Cret's design for the Pan American Union headquarters (now the Organization of American States) in Washington, DC (1908–10),

The McMillan Plan, 1901. Courtesy of the Prints and Photographs Division, Library of Congress. LC-D4-33481, "G 1764" on negative.

became a standard prototype. This approach generated exotic buildings that evolved from the inside out, with classicist formal elements exquisitely juxtaposed with each other.

Distinctions between the two patterns may be hazy. Both were expressions of a New Classicism that created stylistic and functional facilities. And both directly responded to the consolidation of an influential Republican caucus and its possible involvement in such institutions as the US Commission of Fine Arts, which strictly regulated civic works in the United States and overseas. The commission's pseudoacademic, dogmatic function enabled it to dictate visual taste to an American audience eager to expand its aesthetic knowledge.

McKim championed this New Classicism. In addition to the Boston Public Library, he designed improvements to the District of Columbia park system in 1901. Along with Burnham and Frederick Law Olmsted Jr. (1870–1957), principal promoters of the City Beautiful movement, McKim devised a 1902 plan to beautify the urban layout of Washington, DC, that was popularly known as the McMillan Plan, after its champion, Republican senator James McMillan (1838–1902) of Michigan.[13]

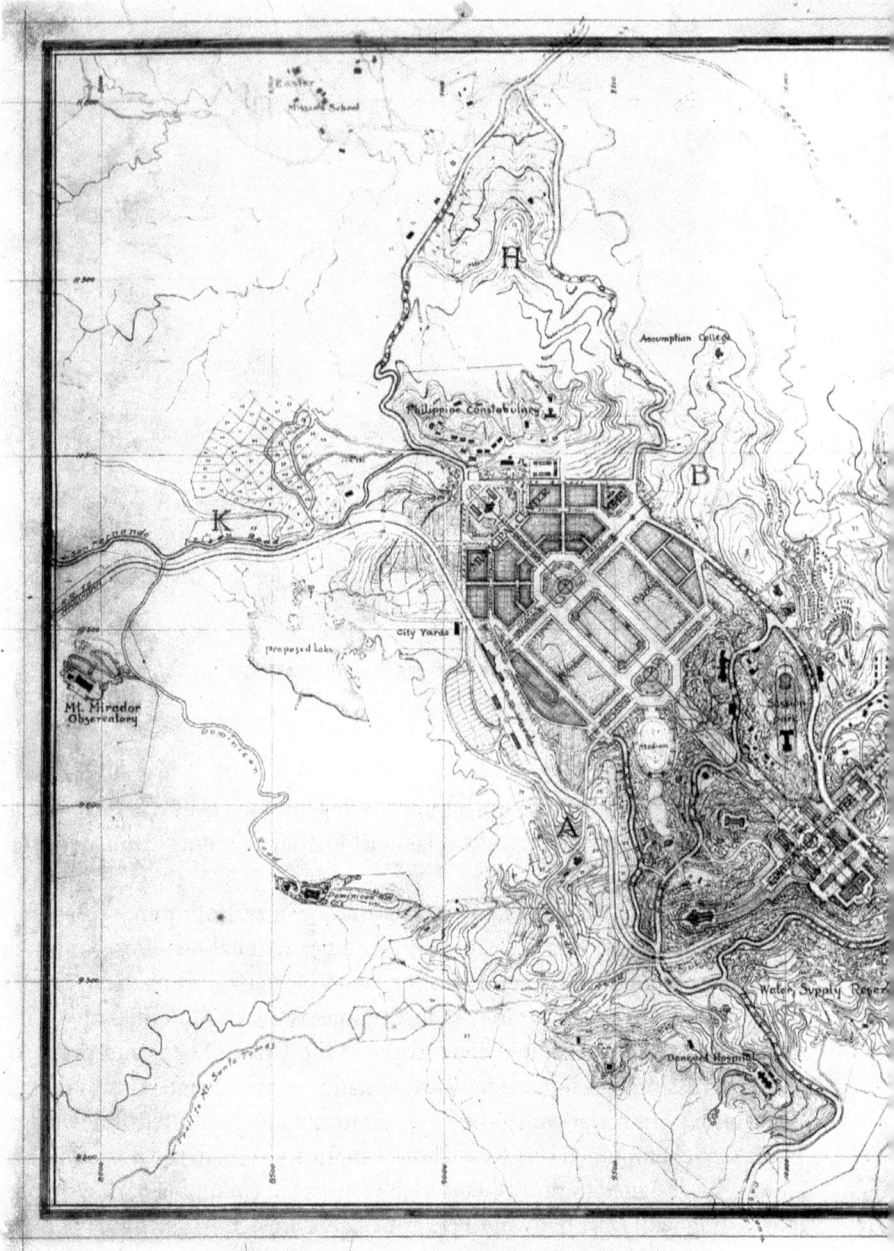

Daniel Hudson Burnham, Plan of Baguio, Philippines, ca. 1905. Courtesy of the Daniel H. Burnham Collection, Ryerson and Burnham Art and Architecture Archive, Art Institute of Chicago. Digital file 194301.080827-02.

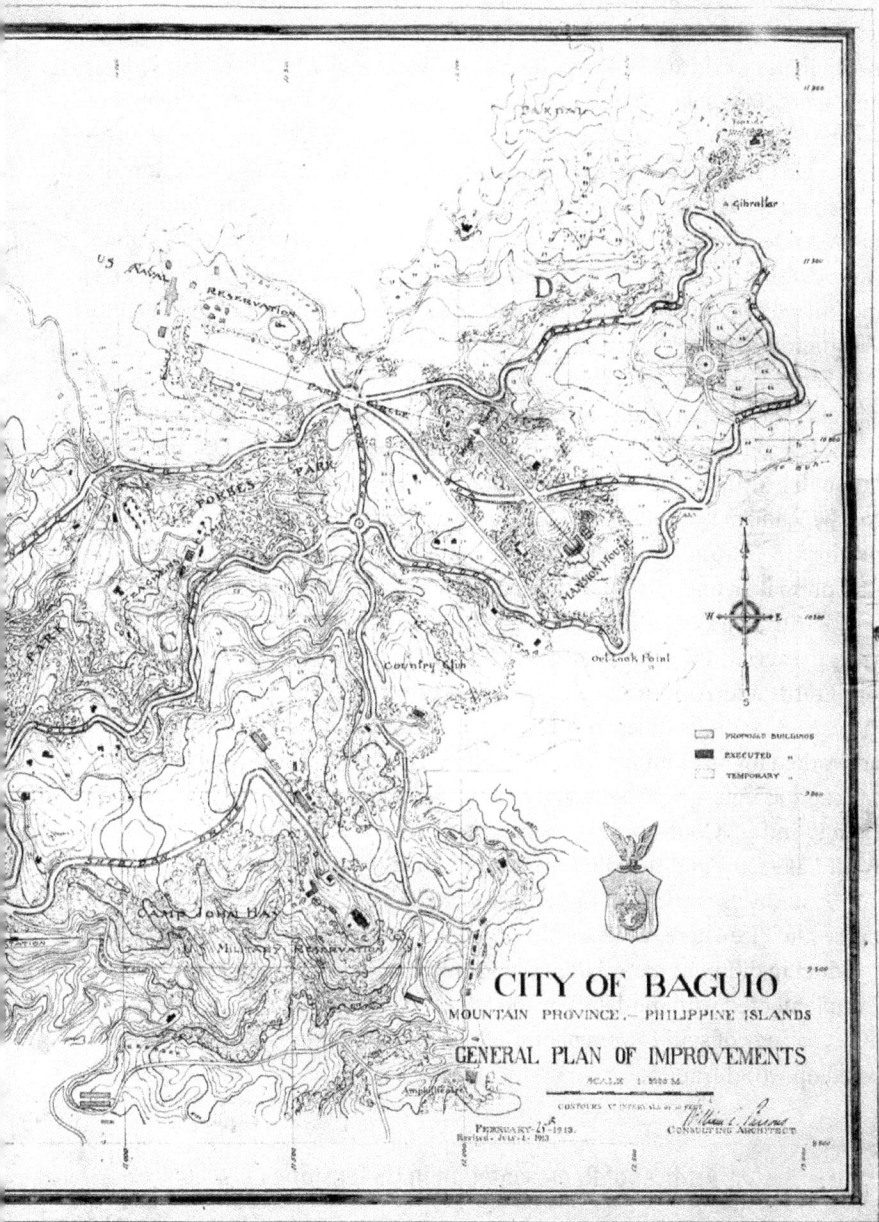

CITY OF BAGUIO

MOUNTAIN PROVINCE,— PHILIPPINE ISLANDS

GENERAL PLAN OF IMPROVEMENTS

SCALE 1: 5000 M.

CONTOURS AT INTERVALS OF 10 FEET

FEBRUARY 21ᵗʰ 1913.
Revised JULY 1- 1913

CONSULTING ARCHITECT

PROPOSED BUILDINGS
EXECUTED "
TEMPORARY "

Other American architects—among them Hunt, Sullivan, Henry Hobson Richardson (1838–86), and Frank Lloyd Wright (1867–1959)—became well known in the world arena. Richardson's, Sullivan's, and Wright's robust stylistic approaches eventually evolved into a contemporary new American architecture.

City Beautiful and its Beaux-Arts works became implanted into new territories via urban arrays of orthogonal grids and boulevards, as the design and construction of the new city of Baguio, the summer capital of the Philippines, demonstrates. Built between 1901 and 1904 under the governorship of William Howard Taft, the city boasted an administrative area that housed central civic amenities. Designed by Burnham, Baguio's layout was akin to that of central Washington, DC.

Other urban and public installations in US-controlled foreign lands alluded to Baguio. For instance, the design and construction of Balboa, at the Panama Canal's Pacific entrance, occurred while Taft was serving as US president. Although Burnham did not design Balboa's Prado, its urban layout was supervised by William Lyman Phillips (1885–1966), Austin Willard Lord (1860–1922), and the US Commission of Fine Arts, Burnham played a notable role as a decision maker, and in 1910 he was appointed as the commission's first chair.

In Latin America, a Europeanized Beaux-Arts strain ran parallel to US efforts to exert its Progressive ethos, with many buildings designed by European immigrants and Americans who received training at the École. Even locals who created such facilities were either alumni of the École des Beaux-Arts or had worked for an alumnus. Thus, mainland US courthouses, post offices, and state capitols mirrored Progressive America overseas, as the Birch Bayh Federal Building and US Courthouse in Indianapolis, the Frank E. Moss US Courthouse in Salt Lake City, and the US Bankruptcy Court in Dayton, Ohio, illustrate.

If Beaux-Arts works had openly associated themselves with the classics in France and elsewhere, what would be expected in US foreign contexts when introducing different materials and design techniques? Would Progressivism be implemented with moderation and restraint, as with the White City, where a few coatings of staff (a concoction of plaster and hemp fibers) were simply pasted on wood framing?

Artifices of Representation in US Territories

What role did rotundas, domes, *salles des pas-perdus*, and anagrams play in the civic architecture of this period? Did they serve only functional purposes—that is, assisting either circulation or natural ventilation? Or did Progressive America use these elements with ulterior, proselytizing intents?

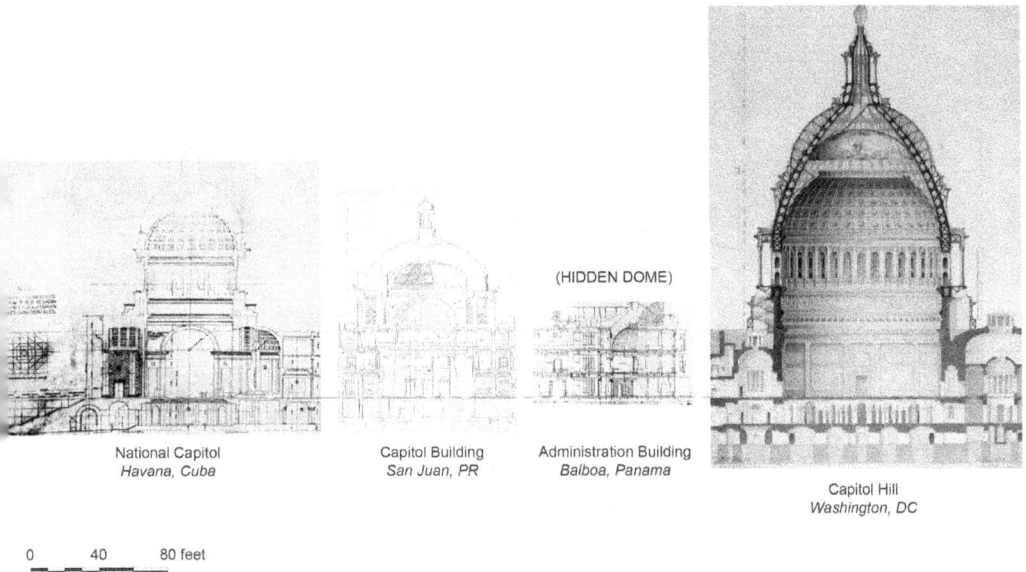

(HIDDEN DOME)

National Capitol
Havana, Cuba

Capitol Building
San Juan, PR

Administration Building
Balboa, Panama

Capitol Hill
Washington, DC

0   40   80 feet

Comparison of domes of US government buildings in Latin America and the US Capitol, Washington, DC. Diagram by author based on building sections from Santovenia, República de Cuba–Capitolio; Architecture Library, University of Puerto Rico, Precinct of Río Piedras; National Archives and Records Administration, College Park, Maryland; and Library of Congress, Washington, DC.

As Beaux-Arts and City Beautiful building components, these showcase elements epitomize a building's exceptionalist memory. One of them, the panorama, summarizes how they still fascinate their audiences.

According to Erkki Huhtamo, panoramas may house a market for mediated realities and (seemingly) emancipated gazes. In other words, bird's-eye views, which started as means of surveillance, eventually became acceptable ways of seeing. The panorama may have mirrored the ambitions of the urban bourgeoisie, but the total number of panorama rotundas was limited, and most people never had an opportunity to experience one firsthand.[14]

Privileged viewers adopted phantasmagoria, or a fascination with the invisible, as a disposition for interpreting their dystopian imagery. Similar artifices of representation conveyed such kind of visuality. According to Huhtamo, the diorama, the cosmorama, the peristrephic panorama, the Apollonicon, and the Euphonon were some of these devices, with Jeremy Bentham's panopticon as an immediate predecessor.[15] All preceded the movie theater, and all fell into oblivion when the film industry superseded still photographs, enhancing the available representational means.

Section of the Rotunda, Leicester Square, 1801. Courtesy of the British Library.

Which thematic displays did these representational tools portray? Bodies of water—a precondition for new towns and cities—became prominent. The 1889 Universal Exposition in Paris, for example, projected a vivid showcase of the Mississippi River. Furthermore, proximity to the ocean became an important topic. The power of Progressive America was greatly indebted to the US Navy and its command of the seas. Such devices also displayed battlefields, with concave surfaces and cylinders buttressing the canvases and encircling the spectators to increase the dystopian effect. One notable example was the Grant Park Civil War Cyclorama in Atlanta. In US territories, public facilities also endorsed phantasmagoria, with milestones and national celebrations such as independence dates and commemorations of the births of notable people becoming common.

Patriotic symbolism infuses the overall design of the rotunda and cupola of the Puerto Rican Capitolio. On its second floor, low reliefs by Leone Tommasi (1903–65) narrate the island's history. Murals and decorations expand on historical eras such as the pre-Columbian era when the Taínos ruled the

Hall of Lost Steps, Capitolio, Havana, Cuba, 1929. Photograph by Carol M. Highsmith. Courtesy of the Prints and Photographs Division, Library of Congress. LC-USZ62-123456.

island; its discovery, conquest, and colonization by Europeans; the configuration of a cabildo; and the abolition of slavery. The rotunda also showcases eight sculptures that symbolize Justice, Liberty, Education, Health, Science, the Arts, Industry, and Agriculture.

At the Cuban Capitolio, the rotunda's floor marks the origin point for all Cuban highways with a gigantic diamond (brillante) at the center of its radial axis. Similarly, the Hall of Lost Steps (Salle des Pas-Perdus) works as an artifice of representation. This 120-meter (394-foot) corridor (also known as the Green Hall) is gilded by thirty-two light fixtures resembling torches. Exquisite green marble columns with bronze bases support the hall's barrel vault, with the rotunda splitting its linear trajectory into two symmetrical halves.

In the rotunda of the Panama Canal Administration Building, the walls are covered with canvas panels that praise the feats of the waterway's construction: the Miraflores locks, the Gatun spillway, a lock miter gate, and the Gaillard Cut, a massive excavation that buried alive dozens of workers and until recently experienced landslides. The frieze is a panorama of a pit from Gaillard Cut. Painted in 1914 by William van Ingen (1858–1955), a successor of Thomas Cole

William van Ingen, mural depicting work at the Gaillard Cut, Panama Canal Administration Building, Balboa, 1915.

(1801–48), Asher Brown Durand (1796–1886), George Inness (1825–94), and the Hudson River School painters, these panels which total 89 square meters (958 square feet) constitute one of the most extensive American landscape paintings outside the United States.

The anagram, another representational tool that is common around the world, is evident in the layout of Balboa. Italian engraver and painter Giovanni Battista Bracelli (fl. 1616–49) alluded to the figure of a warrior for the configuration of a small town in his *Bizarreries* (1624), in which an *alfabeto figurato* overlapped letters with human forms. Cities such as Centuripe in Sicily also ascribed anthropomorphic figures to their urban layouts.

In this context, Lord and Phillips may have incorporated an acronymic anagram in the design of Balboa:

E: a formal allusion to the Administration Building's overall plan configuration ("Estados")
U: enclosed by the letter E, following the building's overall plan configuration ("United," "Unidos")
A: visible from the base of the mountain; a bird's-eye perspective from the rotunda of the
    Administration Building also contains the A ("America")
S: the vertical axis of the Prado; resembles a royal scepter ("States")
C: generated by rotating the letter U ("Canal")

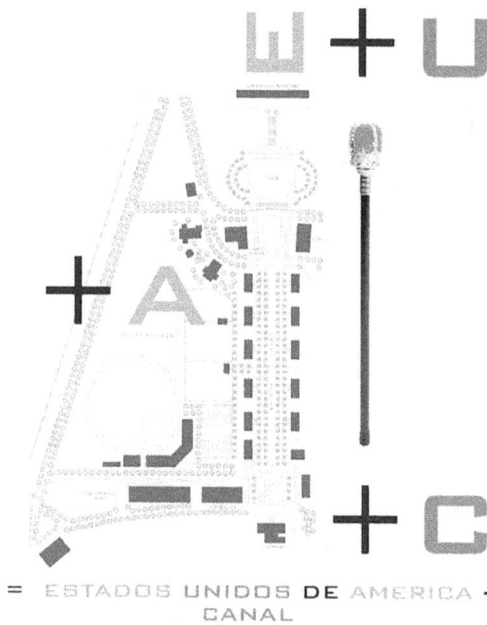

Site layout of the Panama Canal Administration Building. Diagram by author based on drawings from *Canal Record* 9, no. 15 (December 1, 1915): 128. Courtesy of the George A. Smathers Libraries, University of Florida.

Was the proselytizing intent of monumental rotundas, domes, and *salles des pas-perdus* and their visually compelling imagery required to govern US territories? Is a hidden Manifest Destiny still bewildering audiences through these historical artifices of representation as legacies of a foregone era?

Rankin & Kellogg, south (front) facade, Birch Bayh Federal Building and US Courthouse, Indianapolis 1905. Photo by author.

CHAPTER 2

RELEVANT EXAMPLES OF US CIVIC BEAUX-ARTS ARCHITECTURE

The Birch Bayh Federal Building and US Courthouse: A Representative Beaux-Arts Structure from the Tarsney Act Era

The Birch Bayh Federal Building and US Courthouse (originally known as the US Courthouse and Post Office), located in the space bounded by Ohio, Meridian, Pennsylvania, and New York Streets in Indianapolis, became a benchmark for the design and construction of Tarsney Act installations.

According to the GSA's description,

> Resting on a gray granite foundation, the Birch Bayh Federal Building and US Courthouse is a steel-framed, flat-roofed structure clad with Indiana limestone. The south (front) elevation has eleven bays, separated by three-story Ionic engaged columns and flanked by entry pavilions. Each pavilion has a central cast-bronze and glass doorway, reached by a wide, shallow gray granite stair flanked by pedestals.[1]

The building's magnificent decorative features include mosaic-covered ceilings with Roman motifs, coffered ceilings with squares and rosettes, and semicircular domes with stained-glass skylights. The layout of this four-story, U-shaped, symmetrical Beaux-Arts facility includes twin cantilevered marble

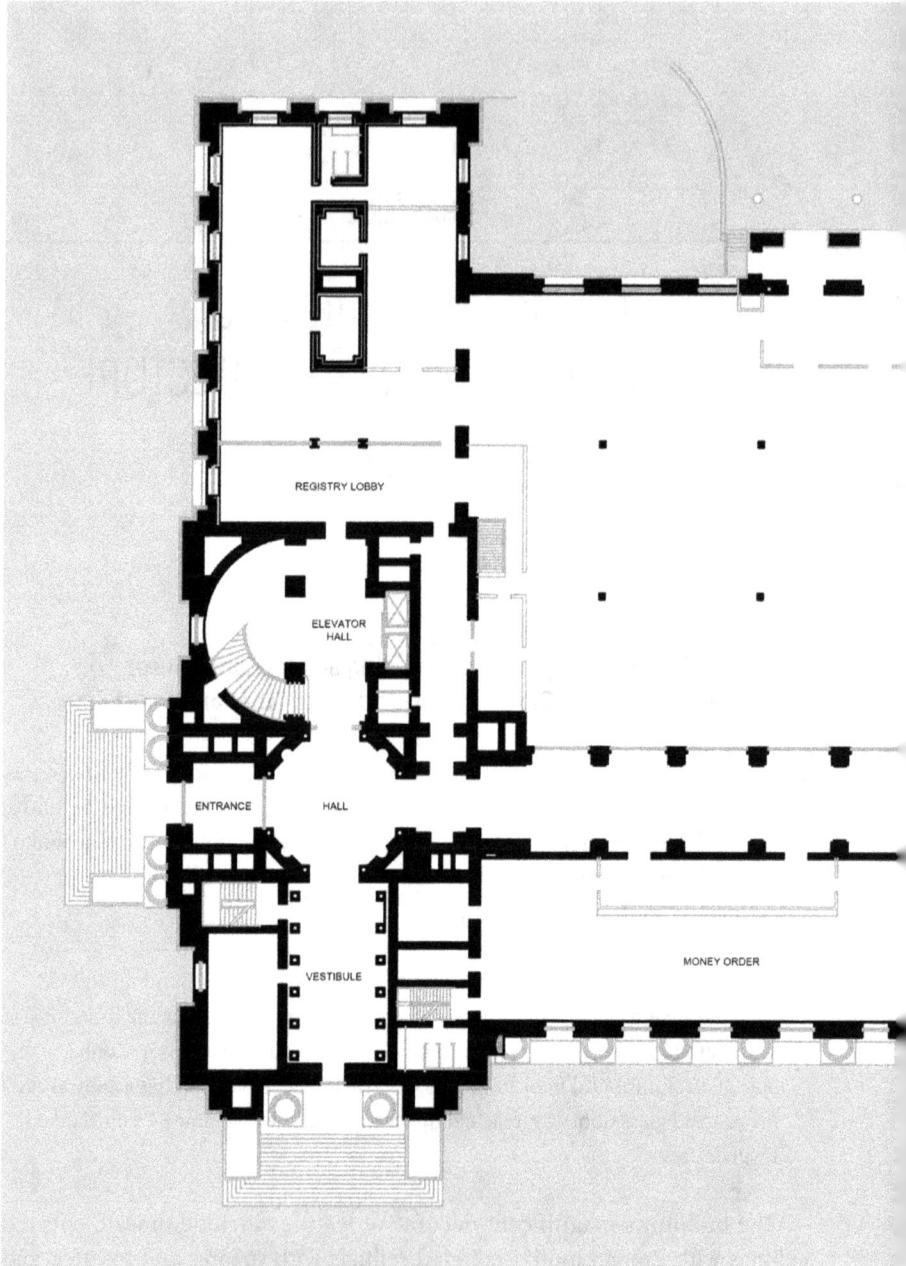

Fourth floor plan, Birch Bayh Federal Building and US Courthouse, Indianapolis, 1905. AutoCAD drawing by author. Courtesy of the US General Services Administration.

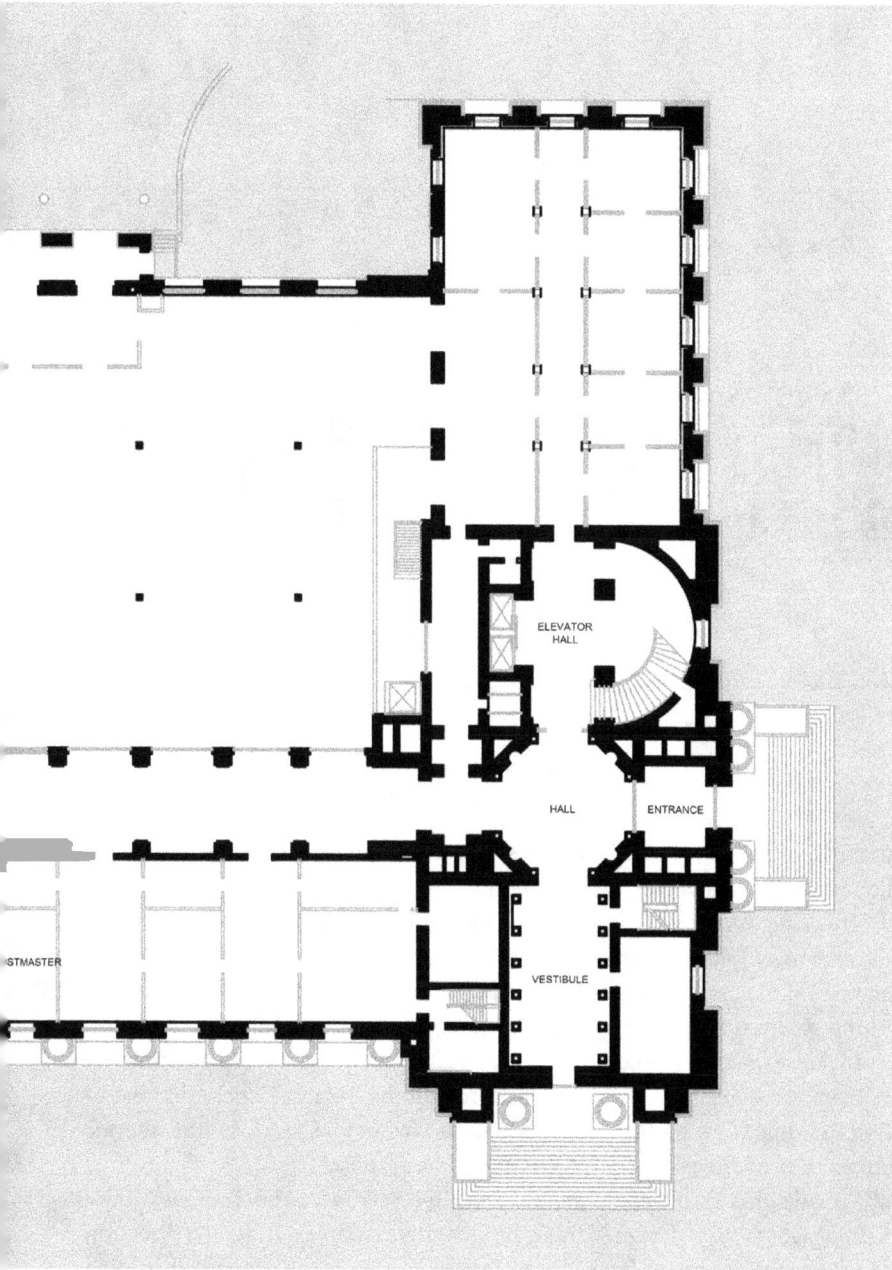

ELEVATOR
HALL

HALL   ENTRANCE

STMASTER

VESTIBULE

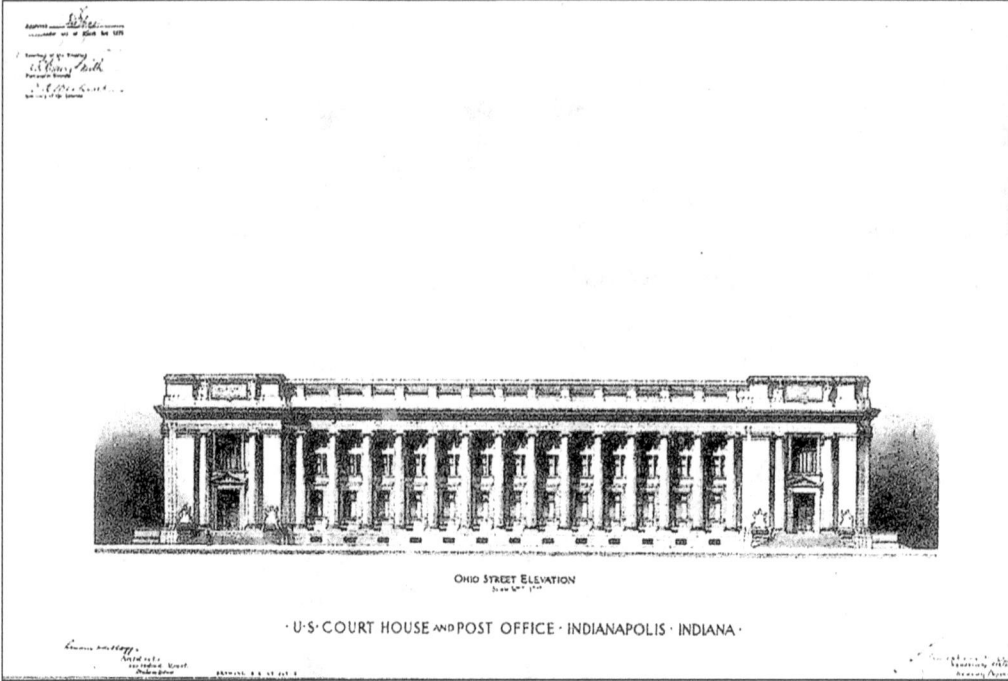

OHIO STREET ELEVATION

· U·S· COURT HOUSE AND POST OFFICE · INDIANAPOLIS · INDIANA ·

Rankin & Kellogg, Birch Bayh Federal Building and US Courthouse, Indianapolis, 1905. Courtesy of the US General Services Administration.

grand stairways with bronze railings that run from the first floor to the third floor at both ends of the original premises.

This US government building uses artwork to allude to its civic functions. For instance, John Massey Rhind's 1908 sculptures at the exterior doorways embody the modern deities of Industry, Science, Agriculture, and Literature. Rhind received a gold medal at the 1904 St. Louis World's Fair.

Inside, exquisitely decorated neoclassical courtrooms feature paintings by William van Ingen (who also painted murals for the Panama Canal Administration Building). The building's north wing, added in 1938, encloses the interior atrium and includes depression-era murals and friezes.

Philadelphia architects John Hall Rankin (1868–1952) and Thomas Moore Kellogg (1862–1935) designed this administrative complex under the direction of supervising architect James Knox Taylor. Rankin and Kellogg had studied architecture at the Massachusetts Institute of Technology. Before opening a firm with Rankin and Edward A. Crane, Kellogg had worked for McKim, Mead & White.

Rankin & Kellogg, Birch Bayh Federal Building and US Courthouse, Indianapolis. Aerial view from Google Earth.

James Knox Taylor, US government building from the World's Fair, St. Louis, 1904.

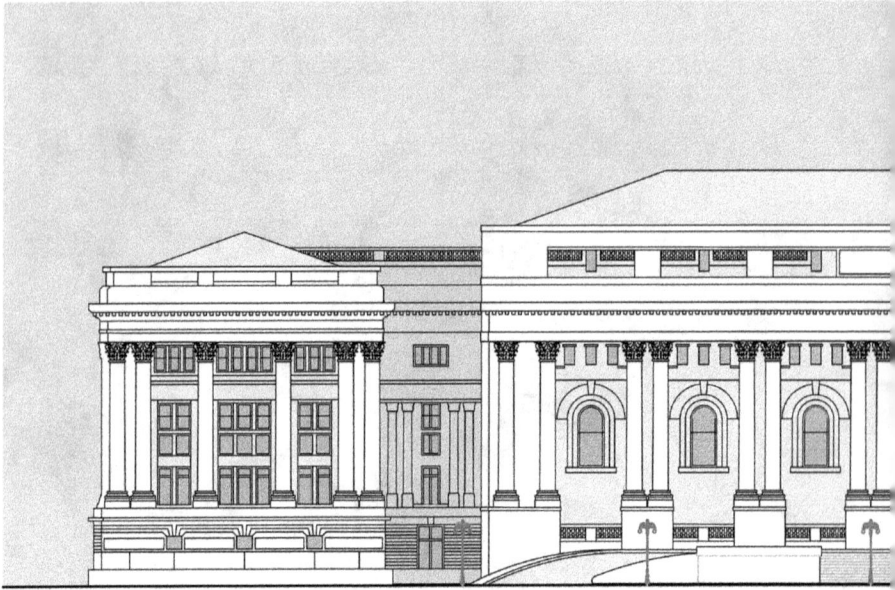

RE

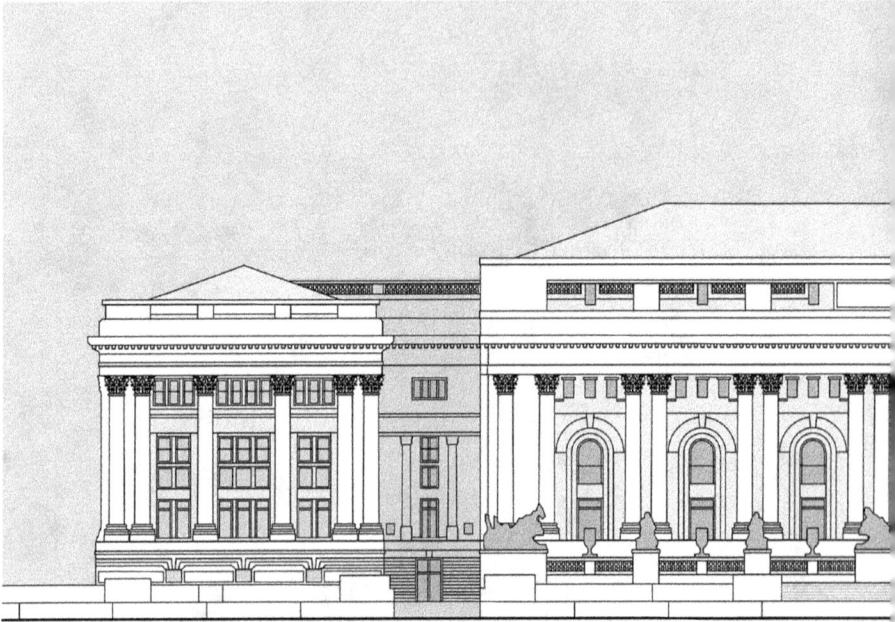

FRO

Lord & Hewlett, facade Proposals for the US Department of Agriculture Administration Building, Washington, DC, 1901. AutoCAD elevations by author from existing drawing. Courtesy of the USDA/ National Agricultural Library.

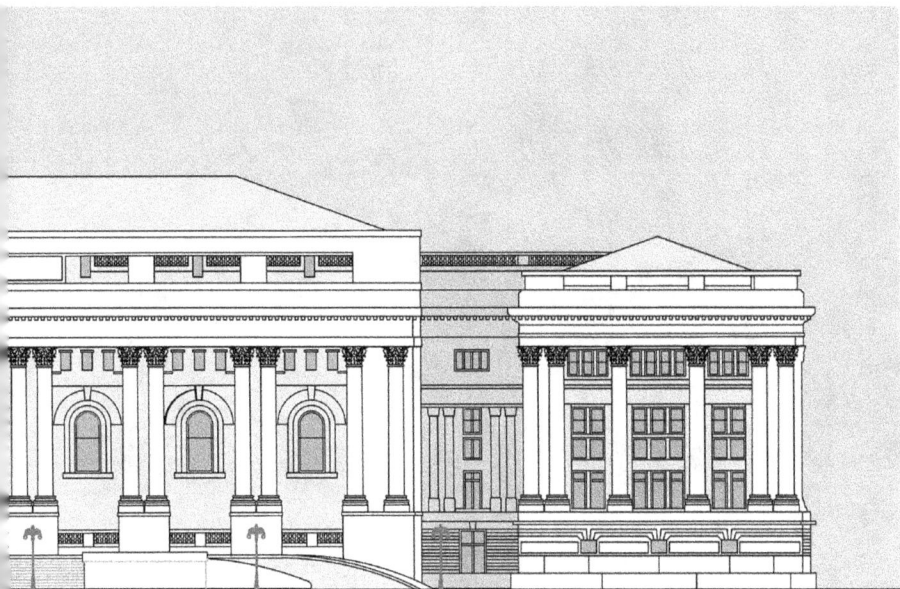

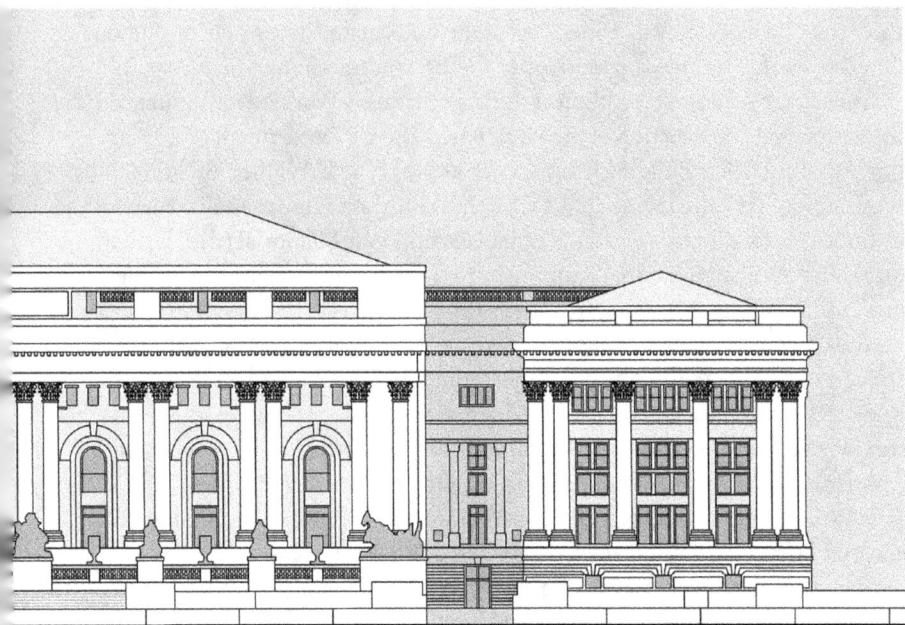

Rankin, Kellogg & Crane, US Department of Agriculture Administration Building, Washington, DC, 1908. Photo by Mr.TinMD, https://www.flickr.com/photos/mr_t_in_dc/2303907816.

New York contractor John Pierce Company built the structure between 1902 and 1905. At the time of its design and construction, Indiana's Charles W. Fairbanks (1852–1918) was a member of the US Senate Committee on Public Buildings and Grounds, a precursor of the US Commission of Fine Arts.

The US Government Building at the 1904 St. Louis World's Fair influenced the design and construction of the Birch Bayh. The US Department of Agriculture Administration Building (now known as the Jamie L. Whitten Building) in Washington, DC, the Indianapolis City Hall (1910), the Indianapolis–Marion County Central Library (1917), the Indiana World War Memorial (dedicated in 1927), and the Panama Canal Administration Building (1914) are other buildings influenced by this structure.

The US Government Building, also designed under Taylor's oversight, became an icon of grandeur and glory, incorporating architectural attributes such as E- or U-shaped partis, exposed or hidden domes, and coffered vestibule and corridor ceilings. Straight entablatures with molded architraves, friezes, and dentils also became significant. Other aesthetic elements included Ionic, Doric, and Corinthian colonnades with squared or fluted columns, exterior doorways encased by pediments, terraced slopes, and curved balusters.

The US Department of Agriculture Administration Building in Washington, DC, resembles government installations from the St. Louis World's Fair. A jury formed by the Senate Park Commission, which included Daniel H. Burnham, Charles F. McKim, Frederick Law Olmsted Jr., and Augustus Saint-Gaudens

President Theodore Roosevelt on a Bucyrus shovel, Panama Canal, 1906. Courtesy of the Granger Historical Picture Archive.

(1848–1907) and was headed by Taylor, opened the design competition in 1901 and ultimately selected the New York City firm of Lord & Hewlett to design and construct the building. However, officials at the Department of Agriculture considered Lord & Hewlett's entry too ornamental. The firm of Rankin, Kellogg & Crane was eventually retained for the project, which opened to the public in 1908. The Isthmian Canal Commission subsequently retained Lord & Hewlett for the Panama Canal Administration Building.

Other Representative Beaux-Arts Structures of the Tarsney Act Era

Other Tarsney Act–era buildings share formal and spatial attributes.

The Frank E. Moss US Courthouse in Salt Lake City is a five-story U-shaped Classical Revival facility at Fourth South and Main Streets in the Exchange Place Historic District. In 1902, Taylor initiated its design supervision.

James Knox Taylor, front facade, Frank E. Moss US Courthouse, Salt Lake City, 1905 (resurfaced in 1932). Photo by author.

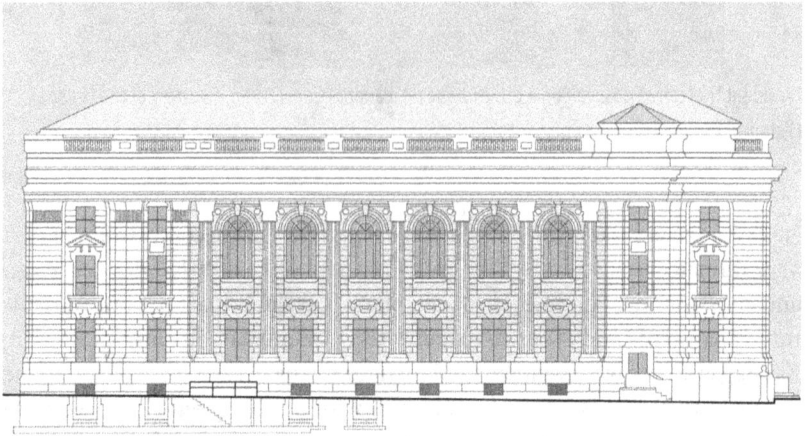

South elevation, Frank E. Moss US Courthouse, Salt Lake City, 1905. AutoCAD drawing by author from existing drawing. Courtesy of the General Services Administration.

View of two-story Ionic columns, James Knox Taylor, US Bankruptcy Court, Dayton, Ohio, 1915. Photo by author.

James Knox Taylor, front facade, US Bankruptcy Court, Dayton, Ohio, 1915. Photo by author.

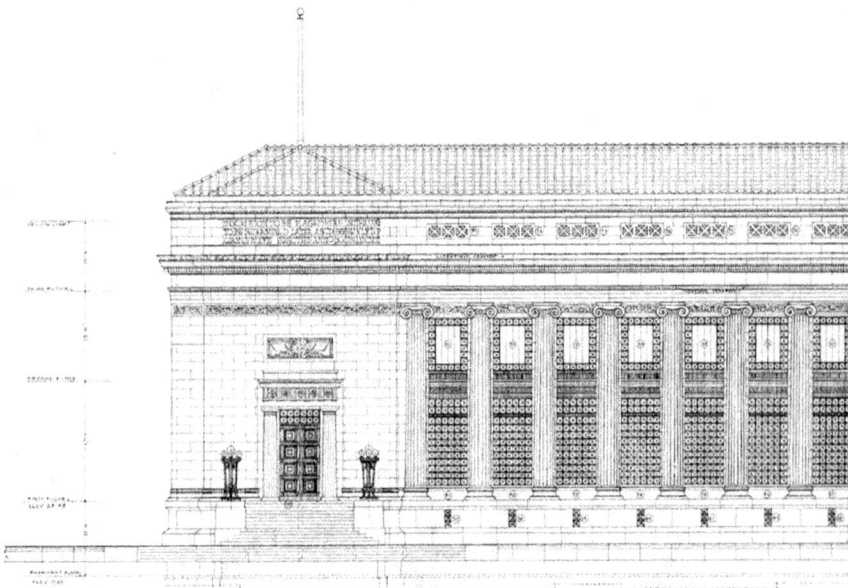

ELEVATION · O

ONE · E I G H T H ·

RETURN TO ROOM 411

Drawer 3047

Third Street elevation, US Bankruptcy Court, Dayton, Ohio, 1915. Courtesy of the General Services Administration.

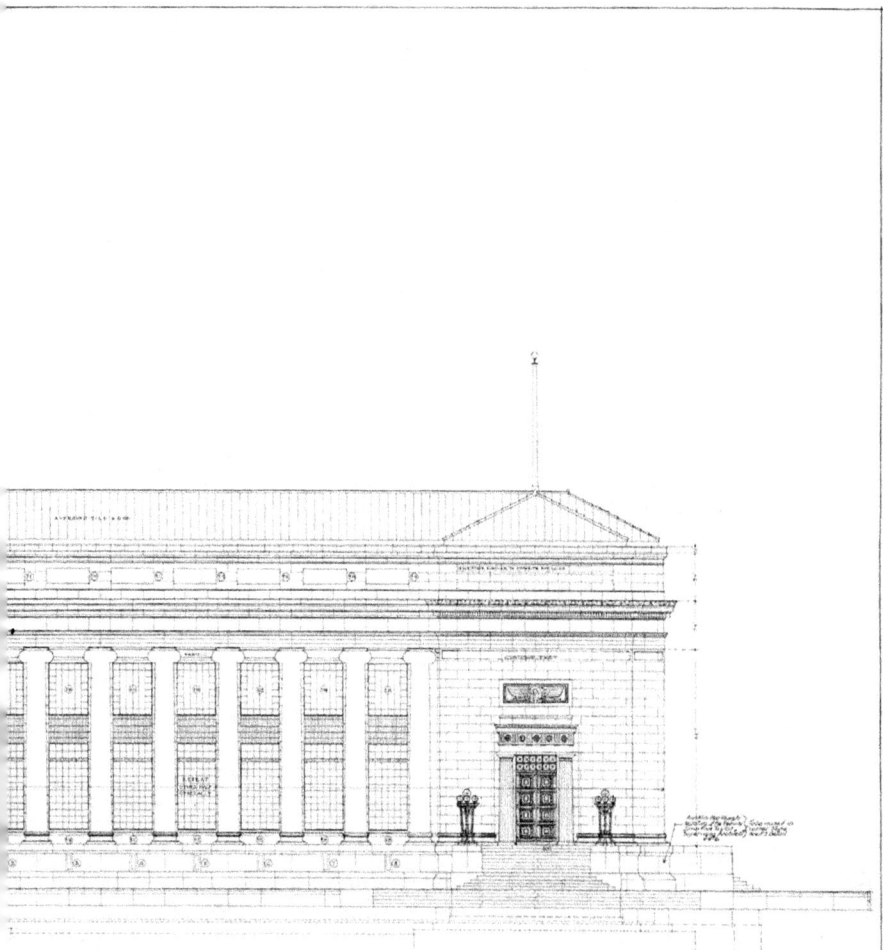

STREET

RETURN TO ROOM 411

U. S. P. O. & CT. H.
DAYTON, OHIO.
Dn'n. by _____ No. 8
Tr'd. by _____
Ch'd by _____

3647   RETURN TO ROOM 411

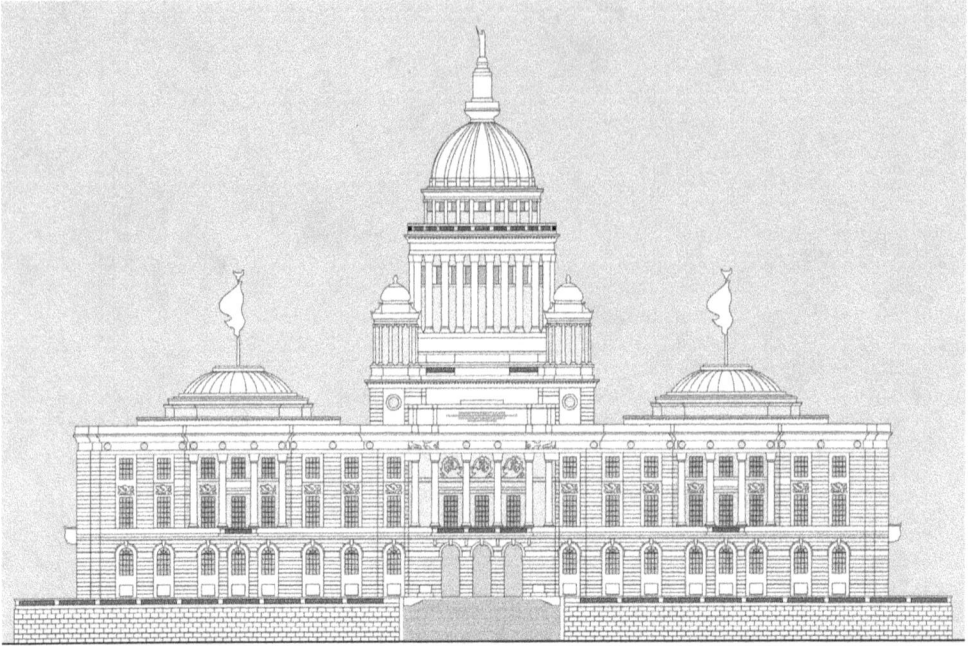

McKim, Mead & White, front facade, Rhode Island Statehouse, Providence, 1895–1904. AutoCAD elevation by author from existing drawing. Courtesy of Rowman & Littlefield.

The building opened in 1905, with additions constructed in 1912 and 1932. The original soft Kyune sandstone exterior experienced cracking and spalling as it settled, and in 1932 the building was clad in gray granite.

Although Utah and the Canal Zone had few things in common, there are formal similarities between the Frank E. Moss Courthouse and the Panama Canal Administration Building and other facilities in US foreign territories. In addition, both the US state and the former territory were also united by an excavating device, the Bucyrus steam shovel, which opened the way for Progressive America.

Taylor also designed another U-shaped Classical Revival structure, the US Bankruptcy Court in Dayton, Ohio, which was built by Philadelphia contractor Herbert B. Knox in 1915. Located at the southeast corner of West Third and Wilkinson Streets, the facility is known to many as the Grecian Lady of Third Street.

Two side entrances flank the building's Ionic Third Street colonnade, directly alluding to such works as the Pan-American Union installations in Washington, DC, by French American architect Paul Cret. New Hampshire granite, stone, ceramic tile, and bronze clad the Dayton courthouse's exterior finishes.

Atrium and dome, Rhode Island Statehouse, Providence, 1895–1904. View of Atrium and Dome. Photo by Bestbudbrian, https://commons.wikimedia.org/wiki/File:Rhode_Island_State_House_-_Atrium_%26_Dome.jpg.

The lobby's ceiling showcases a rich composition of coffered octagons, squares, and rosettes. The structure also features a terrazzo floor trimmed with verde antique marble.

In 1890, Rhode Island began planning construction of a new statehouse, retaining McKim, Mead & White for its design. Constructed between 1895 and 1904, this landmark stands next to Smith Hill in downtown Providence.

Various modifications were made to the plan prior to construction: for instance,

two bays were added to each of the wings, so increasing the length that the central three bays of the wings were enframed with pilasters that repeated the motif of the entrance pavilions. The depth of both entrance pavilions was increased and into the north pavilion the state library was placed on the upper floor. Replacing the monitor domes for the legislative chambers on the original design were low-rising, Roman saucer domes. Finally, on the exterior much of the ornament was simplified and some sculpture eliminated. On the interior, most of the new space went into additional offices. . . . The drama and centrality of the rotunda was increased. Initially projected to be built of either Indiana limestone or Rhode

Exterior view, Capitolio, San Juan, Puerto Rico, 1929. Courtesy of the FSA/OWI Collection, Prints and Photographs Division, Library of Congress. LC-USF34-9058-C.

Island granite, the final material was white Georgia marble. . . . Finally, in 1898, the diameter of the dome was increased by five feet in an attempt to match the size of the Minnesota State Capitol then under construction.[2]

Examples of US Civic Beaux-Arts Architecture in the Americas

Capitolio (Capitol Building), San Juan, Puerto Rico

After the Spanish-American War, legislator, journalist, and poet Luis Muñoz Rivera (1859–1916) became a primary advocate for constructing the Puerto Rican Capitolio. Muñoz Rivera's newspaper, *La Democracia*, became one of his best-known accomplishments.

At the time, as a US territory, Puerto Rico convoked a local plebiscite to determine the island's geopolitical status, and La Democracia stood as a bastion for Puerto Rican autonomy. In 1907, Muñoz Rivera introduced a bill "for the erection of an insular building to be known as the Capitol of Puerto Rico

Aerial view, Capitolio, San Juan, Puerto Rico. Google Earth.

in which shall be lodged the Executive Council, the House of Delegates and the Supreme Court."[3]

Before the Capitolio opened, the Legislative Assembly met in the Provincial Delegation Building (which currently houses the Puerto Rican Department of State). Secretary of the interior for Puerto Rico Laurence Grahame (1867–1918) opened the competition to design a new capitol, and the US government provided $3 million for design and construction.

In addition members of the Puerto Rican cabinet such as Muñoz Rivera, Grahame, and the president of the supreme court, José S. Quiñones (1838–1909), the design commission included three architects from the US mainland: E. B. Homer (d. 1929), John E. Howe (d. 1908), and Bowen Bancroft Smith (1869–1932).

A design committee led by William F. Willoughby, president of the Executive Council of Puerto Rico, reviewed more than one hundred proposals for the Capitolio from firms in the United States, Canada, France, Spain, Cuba, and Puerto Rico, selecting three US projects as finalists and initially awarding the

East elevation, Capitolio, San Juan, Puerto Rico, 1929. AutoCAD rendition by author from existing drawing. Courtesy of the Colección Capitolio de Puerto Rico, Archivo de Arquitectura y Construcción de la Universidad de Puerto Rico.

project to the proposal by Frank E. Perkins (b. 1870) featured a flattened central saucer dome with bilateral wings spreading symmetrically from the rotunda. However, the jury later disqualified Perkins's plan because he had attached an inappropriate slogan to the blueprints and selected a design by local architect Carlos del Valle Zeno (1881–1965). The project was put on hold during World War I, and when the Puerto Rican government resumed the project in 1920, it returned to Perkins's alternative, though contributions from multiple architects were eventually incorporated.

In 1919, employees of the Puerto Rican Department of the Interior Francisco Roldán (1890–1988) and Pedro de Castro Besosa (1895–1936), submitted a Spanish Renaissance Revival design. A year earlier, de Castro had become the first Puerto Rican to graduate from a US school of architecture (Syracuse University). Among his projects were the Central High School in Santurce, Puerto Rico (1919–25); the Recreational Center in Santiago de los Caballeros, Dominican Republic (1929); and the Miami Building, also in Santurce (1935).

After years of revised budgets and design proposals, the Puerto Rican government retained architects Rafael Carmoega (1894–1968), Joseph O'Kelly (d. 1970), William Schimmelpfennig (1895–1957), Harry Pembleton (1890–1961), Albert B. Nichols, Luis F. Pina, and Gonzalo Fernós Maldonado (1887–1966). Carmoega's construction documents incorporated elements from Perkins's design, including his semirecessed saucer dome.

Carmoega was born in Ponce, Puerto Rico, and graduated from the Cornell University School of Architecture (1918). He became director of the Architectural Division of Puerto Rico's Department of the Interior and the first Puerto Rican to serve as state architect (1921–36). In addition to the Capitolio and the University of Puerto Rico Main Campus at Río Piedras, other Carmoega projects include Ponce's Mercado de las Carnes (1926), the School of Tropical Medicine (1926), and the Mayagüez City Hall (1926), all of which are listed on the National Register of Historic Places. Beaux-Arts, Spanish Baroque, and Neo-Mudéjar allusions became prevalent in his buildings.

Puerta de Tierra was selected for the site of Puerto Rico's Capitolio. This inland gateway, located near the coastline of Old San Juan, was a remnant of the city walls built during the Spanish conquest. One mile away is the twenty-five-acre Luis Muñoz Rivera Park, which opened to the public in 1936 and features elegant *faux bois* (false wood) objects cast and sculpted by Puerto Rican artist Víctor Cott (1899–1962).

The capitol's initial design covered a surface of nearly fifty-two thousand square feet. The building has three above-ground floors plus an ample basement, and its twin north and south entrances overlook Muñoz Rivera and Ponce de León Avenues. Eight Corinthian columns flank its main porticos, while its wings feature Ionic columns. Entrance doors representing the island's seven senatorial districts at the time, connect the main porticos to the rest of the facility. Adjacent stately areas and monuments also garnish this Capitoline Italian Renaissance Revival structure.

The capitol's dome and entrances resemble the Low Memorial Library at Columbia University, designed by McKim, Mead & White in 1895. Completion of the Capitolio dome took place in 1961.

The dome divides the Puerto Rican Capitolio into two symmetrical wings. A lantern crowns its cupola. Barrel vaults cover the bilateral corridors that connect the rooms and offices, and ornamented semicircular lights top the access doors. Marble staircases flanked by marble columns convey visitors from the first to the second floor. Other fluted columns also complement the decor of the rotunda. Elevators occupy the corners of the square containing the rotunda's circular plan. At the center of the rotunda rests the Puerto Rican Constitution, overlooked by Puerto Rico's coats of arms inside the rotunda's dome.

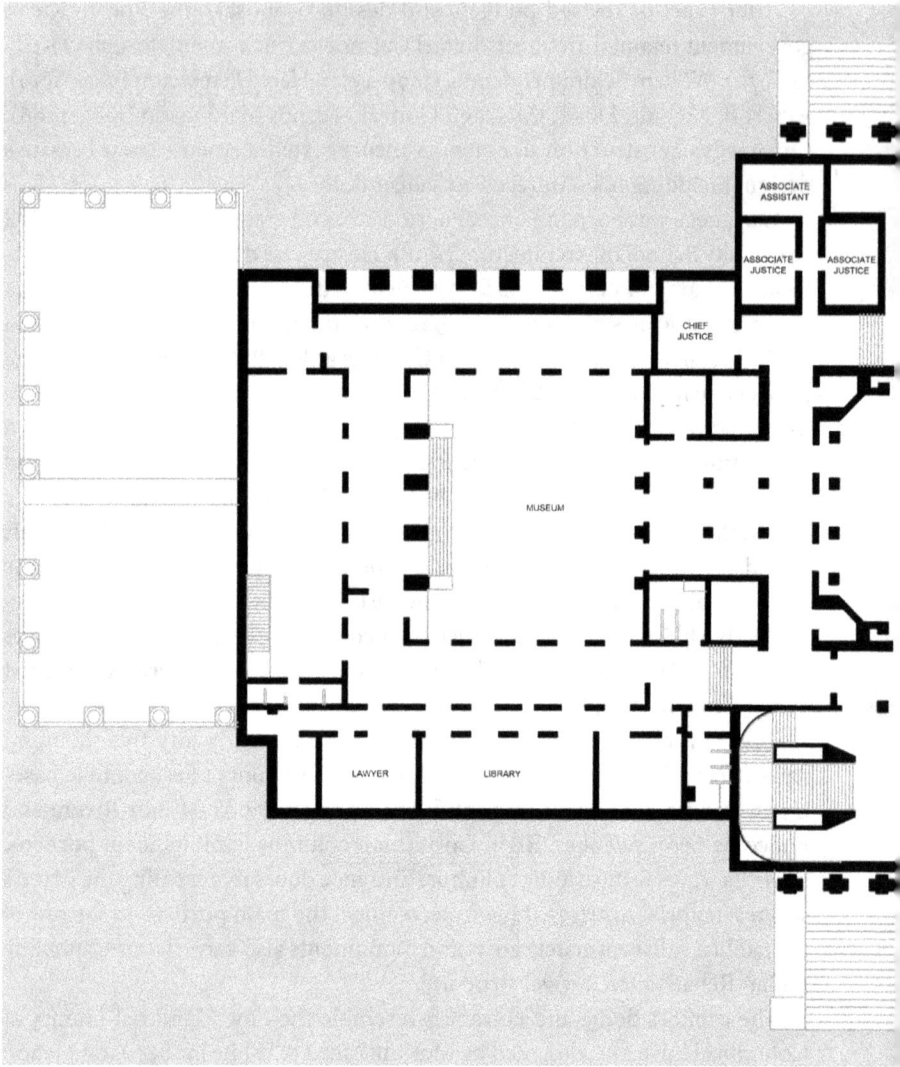

Ground floor plan, Capitolio. San Juan, Puerto Rico, 1929. AutoCAD drawing by author. From Andrés Mignucci, *[Con]Textos*, 60.

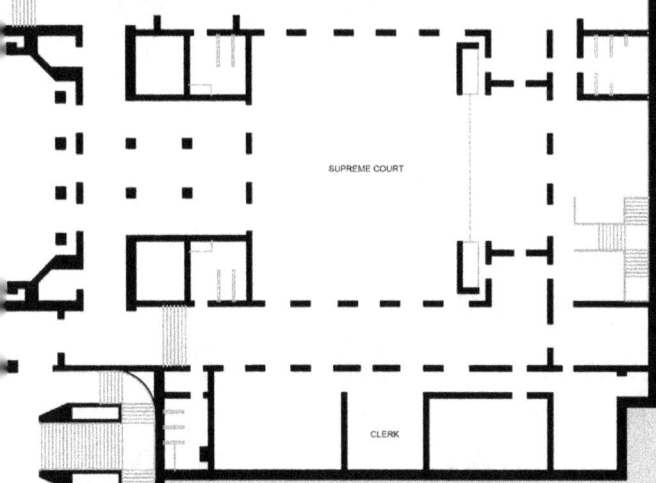

ASSOCIATE
ASSISTANT

ASSOCIATE
JUSTICE

ASSOCIATE
JUSTICE

SUPREME COURT

CLERK

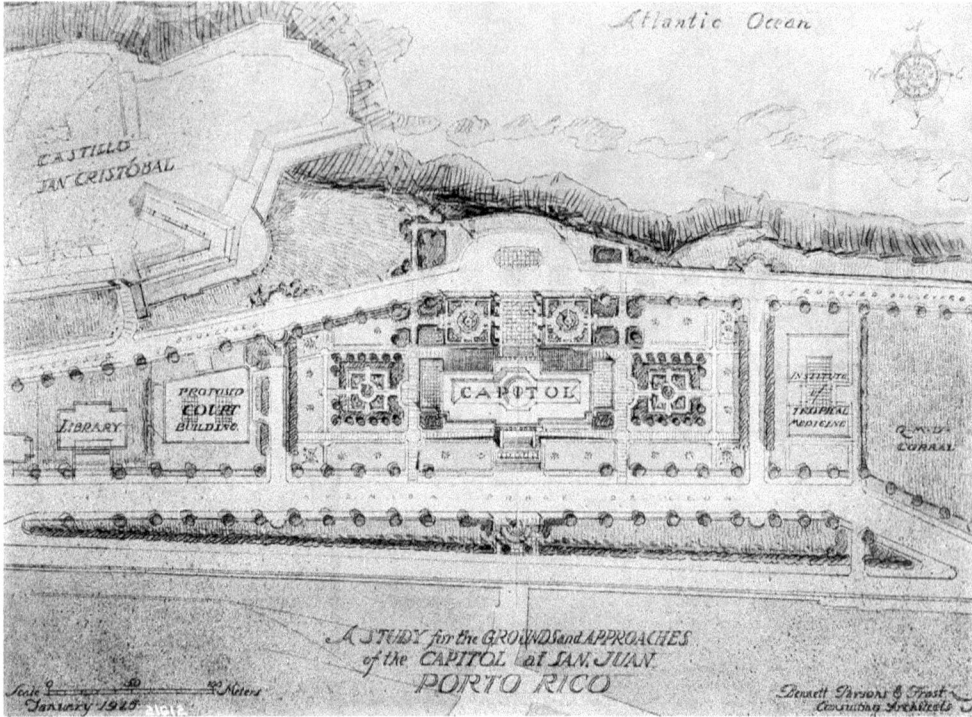

Bennett, Parsons & Frost, Capitolio master plan and Luis Muñoz Rivera Park, San Juan, Puerto Rico, 1925.
Courtesy of the Newberry Library.

The architectural firm of Bennett, Parsons & Frost, formed by Edward H. Bennett (1874–1954), William E. Parsons (1872–1939), and Harry T. Frost (1886–1943), designed both the Capitolio's Master Plan (1925) and the Luis Muñoz Rivera Park (1925). Bennett was educated at the École des Beaux-Arts and was a pioneer in urban design and city planning who had coauthored the Plan of Chicago (1909). Parsons, a graduate of Yale University as well as the École des Beaux-Arts, had previously worked for the Bureau of Public Works in the Philippines (1905–14), where his projects included the Philippine General Hospital (1910), the Manila Hotel (1912), and the Paco Railway Station (1915). Parsons's earlier assignments in the Philippines may have influenced Puerto Rican authorities to retain his firm for urban and landscape design projects.

Parsons had extensive experience in tropical architecture. He favored concrete over other construction materials and commonly used canopies, arcades, and colonnades for weatherproofing. In addition, his firm recommended the use of tropical flora in its landscape designs.

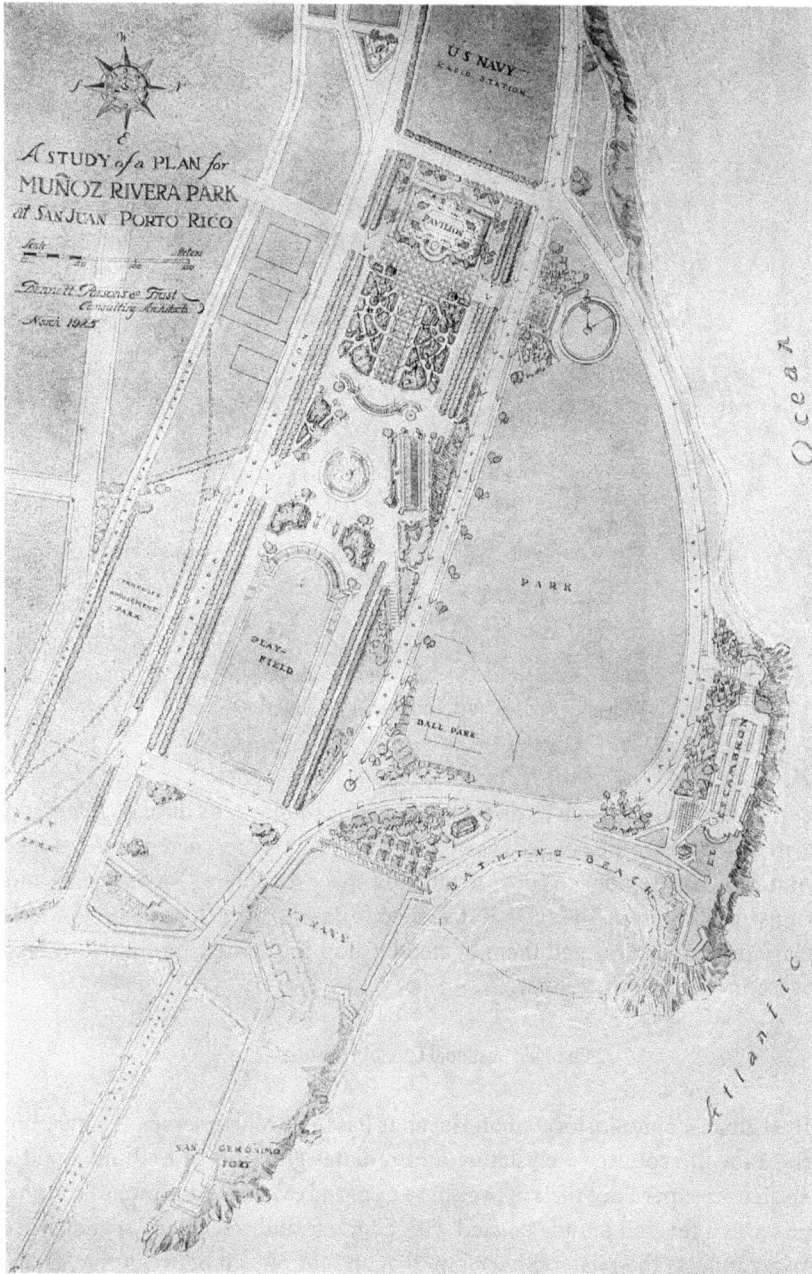

Bennett, Parsons & Frost Capitolio master plan and Luis Muñoz Rivera Park, San Juan, Puerto Rico, 1925. Courtesy of the Newberry Library.

William E. Parsons, 1911. Courtesy of the Newberry Library.

The Capitolio opened its doors to the public in 1929. The local architectural firm of Toro-Ferrer designed two annexes (1952–55) constructed by developer Antonio Díaz Texidor to provide meeting space for Puerto Rico's Senate and House of Representatives. Dr. Rafael Picó (1912–98), director of Puerto Rico's Planning Bureau, located them bilaterally atop the gardens proposed in 1925 by Bennett, Parsons & Frost.

Capitolio (National Capitol), Havana, Cuba

The Cuban Capitolio, located on Havana's Paseo de Martí, serves as a meeting place for the country's legislature and radiates glimpses of monumentality. Audiences experience their approach to its grand exterior staircase as if getting closer to a revered temple erected with concrete and steel. Such spatial symmetry reflects the bilateral harmony that should prevail between the Senate and its chambers.

Built on a site originally occupied by the Villanueva train station (owned by the Havana Central Railway Company), this 39,000-square-meter

Angelo Zanelli, Statue of the Republic, Capitolio, Havana, Cuba, 1929. Courtesy of the University of Notre Dame.

(420,000-square-foot) landmark is 36 meters (118 feet) wide and is highlighted by a 16-meter- (52-foot-) high portico with twelve Ionic granite columns and a frieze engraved with the word Capitolio. The magnificent rotunda is crowned by a drum girdled by multiple columns, or first peristyle, with sixteen ornamental veins articulating the dome.

The cupola is topped by a lantern, or second peristyle, supported by ten Ionic columns; it resembles Jacques-Germain Soufflot's Panthéon in Paris and indirectly Donato Bramante's Tempietto in Rome. Two Doric colonnades flank the Capitolio's portico, and each colonnade contains a loggia, which works as the preamble to the Hall of Lost Steps.

The Capitol encloses two central courtyards, with the Senate chamber at the end of one wing and the House chamber at the end of the other. A statue of the Republic, inspired by the Greek goddess of wisdom, Pallas Athena, and

Capitolio, Havana, Cuba, 2007. Photo by Yomangani, https://commons.wikimedia.org/wiki/
File:Capitolio_full.jpg.

designed and built by Italian sculptor Angelo Zanelli (1879–1942), measures 15 meters (49.5 feet) high and is located at the end of the rotunda that is bisected by an apse. Zanelli also created two complementary figures, the Tutelary Virtue and the Work, that flanking the entrance and staircase. One of the courtyards contains the mystical sculpture of the Fallen Angel, which bewilders both visitors and locals.

Multiple decorative sculptures, friezes, high reliefs, and metopes exalt allegories to Agriculture, Industry, Commerce, Labor, Family, the Arts, Science, and Progress. Low relief panels crown the main entrance doors, depicting such motifs as the destructive spirit of war, the constructive guardian of peace, and Cuba's coat of arms. Cuban artists Juan José Sicre (1898–1974), Esteban Betancourt (1893–1942), Alberto Sabas, and Lithuanian artist León Droucker (1867–1944) sculpted its friezes and reliefs. Its main doors, of ornamental bronze, were forged by another Cuban artist, Enrique García Cabrera (1893–1949).

According to Arquitectura Cuba, after a brief halt in 1921, architects Eugenio Rayneri Piedra (1883–1960), Félix Cabarrocas Ayala (1887–1961), and Evelio Govantes Fuertes (1886–the 1960s) began working on the project. Rayneri Piedra, who received a strict Beaux-Arts training and in 1904 became the first graduate of the School of Architecture at the University of Notre Dame, in

Aerial view, Capitolio, Havana, Cuba. Google Earth.

South Bend, Indiana, also worked on Cuba's presidential palace and congressional residence.

Cabarrocas Ayala, who was also a sculptor and draftsperson, received an architecture degree from the University of Havana in 1910. He and Govantes Fuertes opened a firm, Govantes y Cabarrocas, that not only finished Rayneri's Capitolio but received other commissions in Havana, including the Hospital General Freyre de Andrade (1916) and the Ludgardita housing complex (1929). For the Capitolio, Cabarrocas and Govantes adopted a Classical Revival style, using McKim, Mead & White's 1895–1904 plans for the Rhode Island Statehouse as a direct referent. The firm also designed the Cuban Pavilion at the Ibero-American Exposition in Seville, Spain (1929), the City Children's Hospital in Havana's Vedado neighborhood (ca. 1940; demolished in the 2010s), and the José Martí National Library (1952–57) at the Plaza de la Revolución in Havana.

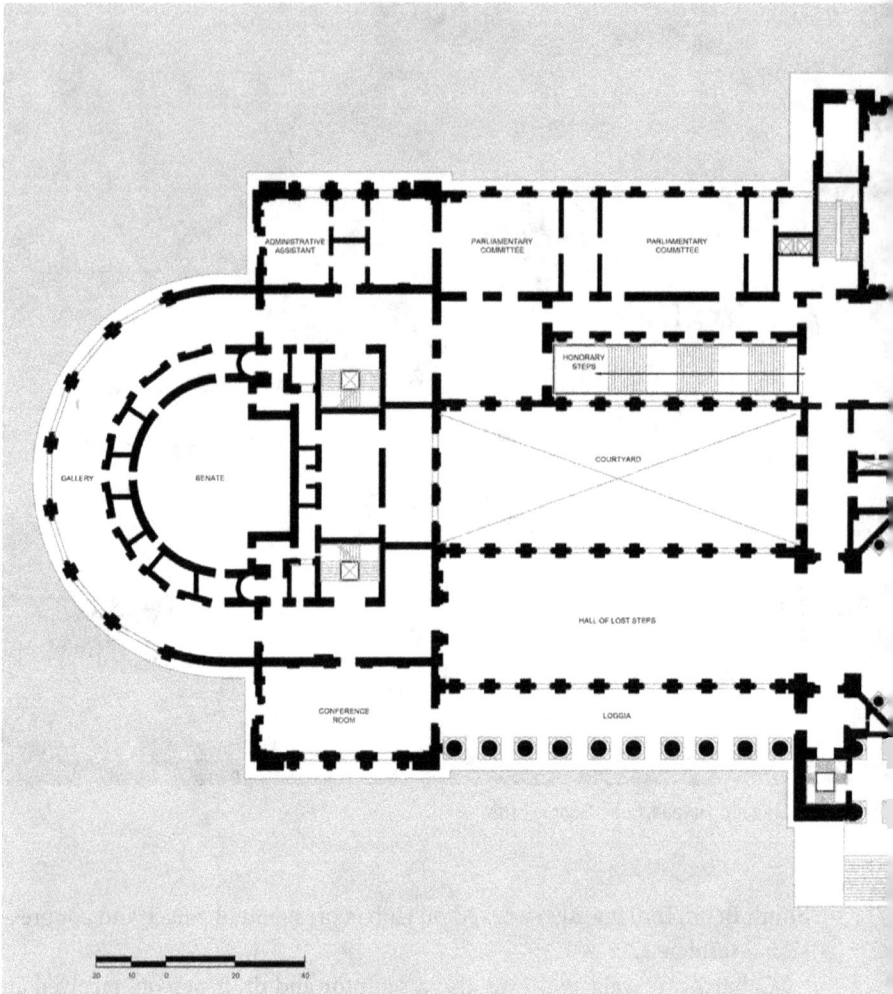

Floor plan, Capitolio, Havana, Cuba, 1929. AutoCAD drawing by author. From María Martín Z. and Rodríguez F. Eduardo, *La Habana*, 140.

Cuban architects José Bens Arrarte (b. 1893) and Pedro Martínez Inclán (1883–1957) also incorporated countless modifications to this project. Raúl Otero of the Cuban Bureau of Public Works worked as a consulting architect. French landscape architect Jean-Claude Nicolas Forestier (1861–1930) designed its gardens.

The construction firm founded by Corydon Tyler Purdy (1859–1944) and Lightner Henderson (1866–1916) supervised and executed the construction of the Cuban Capitolio. Purdy & Henderson opened a Havana branch in 1889 and went on to erect the Banco Nacional de Cuba (1907), the Lonja del Comercio

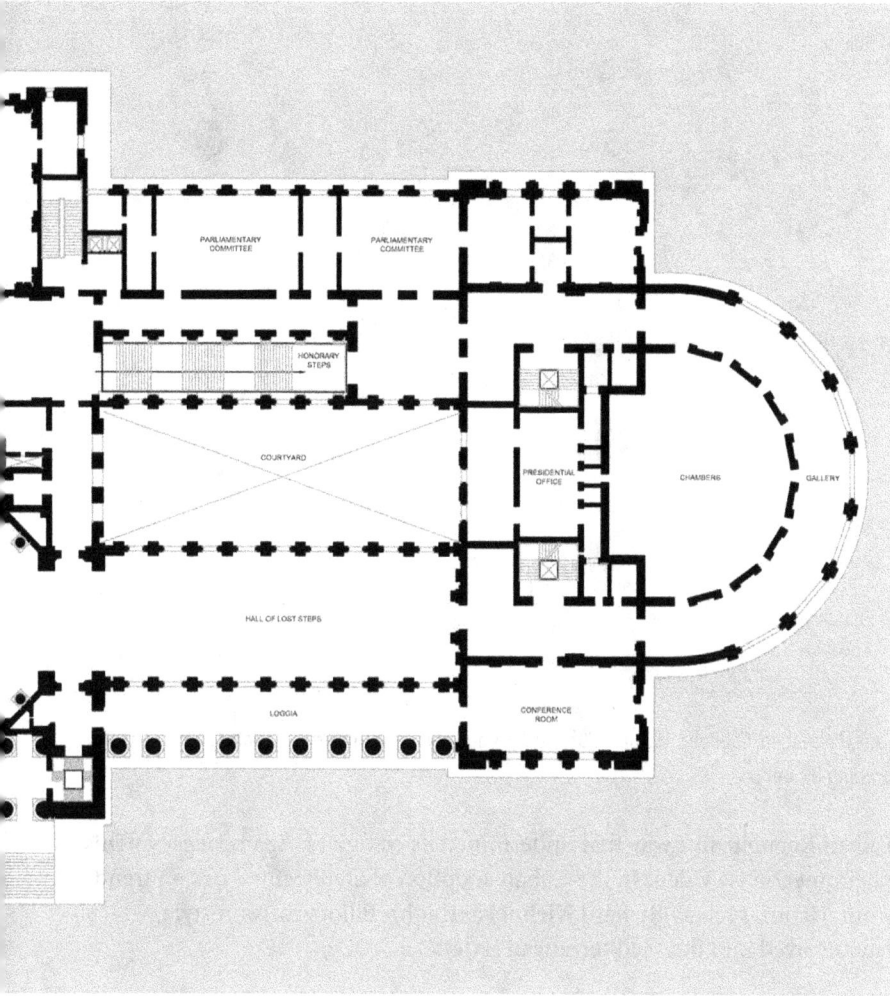

(1909), the Centro Gallego (1915), and the Hotel Nacional (1930). New York City's William Baumgarten & Co. took charge of the Capitolio's steelwork, while British firm Waring and Gillow oversaw the interior decoration.

The Sixth International Conference of American States (Pan-American Conference) took place in Havana in 1928, accelerated the Capitolio's completion date, and the building and gardens opened to the public the following year.

In the wake of the Spanish-American War and the ensuing US military occupation, which lasted until 1902, US Progressivism influenced the young

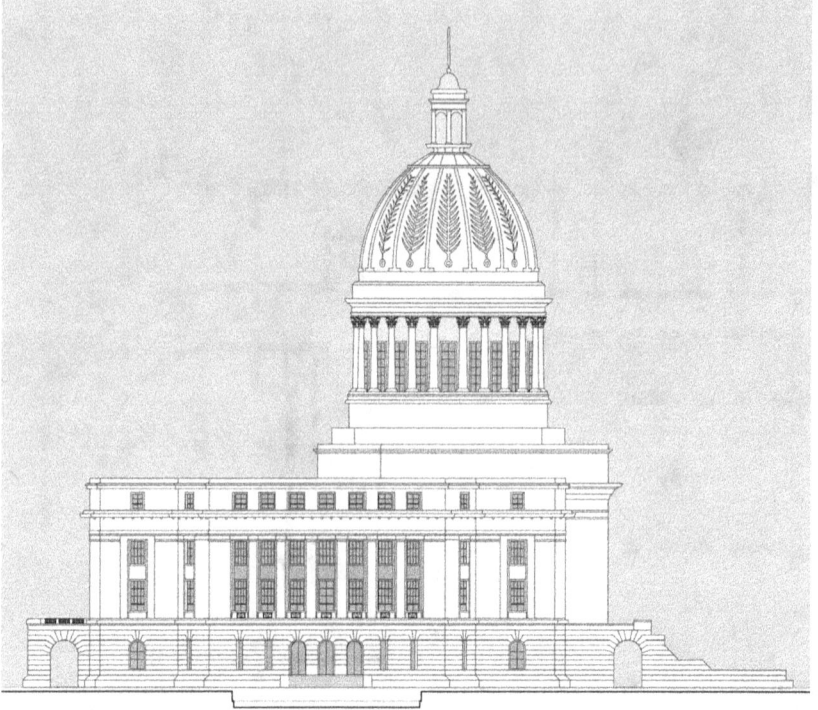

Lateral elevation, Capitolio, Havana, Cuba, 1929. Courtesy of the University of Notre Dame. AutoCAD drawing by author.

Cuban Republic in a way that undermined its colonial Hispanic legacy.[4] This phenomenon is evident in the Cuban adoption of architectural design trends from Miami, such as Richard Kiehnel and John Elliot's mission style, which later evolved into the Mediterranean style.

Palacio Nacional (National Palace), Santo Domingo, Dominican Republic

Concerned that Germany would use the Dominican Republic as its bastion during World War I, the United States occupied the island nation in 1916. For the next eight years, the US Bureau of Insular Affairs oversaw the country's administration. When Félix Lluberes (1898–1988), a wealthy resident of Santo Domingo, donated a 25,000-square-meter (269,000-square-foot) plot for the construction of the University of Saint Thomas Aquinas, the bureau, headed by William E. Pulliam, appropriated the property to serve as the site of its local headquarters, the General Customs Receivership.

When the US occupation ended in 1924, the Dominican government remodeled the building to serve as the country's presidential mansion. The mansion

Interior view, Palacio Nacional, Santo Domingo, Dominican Republic, 1947. From Checo et al., *National Palace*.

Main entrance, Palacio Nacional, Santo Domingo, Dominican Republic, 1947. From Checo et al., *National Palace*, 107.

Exterior view, General Customs Receivership, Santo Domingo, Dominican Republic, ca. 1920. From Checo et al., *National Palace*, 63.

was eventually demolished and replaced by the Palacio Nacional. The administration of President Rafael L. Trujillo Molina (1891–1961) constructed the Palacio Nacional at a cost of 1.5 million pesos between 1944 and 1947 under the guidance of Italian-Dominican engineer Guido D'Alessandro (1895–1954), a 1925 graduate of the Polytechnic Institute of Turin. The design also included professional collaboration with Puerto Rican–born architect Benigno de Trueba Suárez (1877–1948) and Dominican engineers Henry Gazón Bona (1909–1982) and Humberto Ruíz Castillo (1895–1966).

Totaling 18,000 square meters (194,000 square feet), the three-story Palacio Nacional was intended to serve as the government headquarters as well as the presidential residence. On the ground floor were "the offices of the Secretariats of State of the Presidency and Foreign Affairs . . . as well as the administration, the switchboard, the postal and telegraph services of the building, the offices of the Presidential Military Aides, storerooms, deposits, filing rooms," and the like. On the second floor were "the offices of the Secretariats of State of the Presidency and Foreign Affairs and the offices of

erial view, Palacio Nacional, Santo Domingo, Dominican Republic. Google Earth.

the President." The third floor housed the president's residence; "the Grand Activity Room, called Trujillo Room"; and "a large salon bar with spacious terraces for buffet service, etc."[5] It still houses the executive branch of the Dominican government.

The building features Ionic and Corinthian classical columns, two central courtyards that provide ventilation, interior balustrades, and interior finishes of marble, bronze, iron, steel, plaster, and mahogany from the centennial period. In addition to an imposing entrance flanked by lions, the Palacio is noteworthy for its monumental staircase and the magnificent dome, which measures 18 meters (59 feet) wide and 34 meters (112 feet). Located at the center of the vestibule, the dome divides the edifice into two quasi-symmetrical wings: the Caryatids or Mirror Room, with multiple female busts adorning its door and mirror frames, and the chapel.

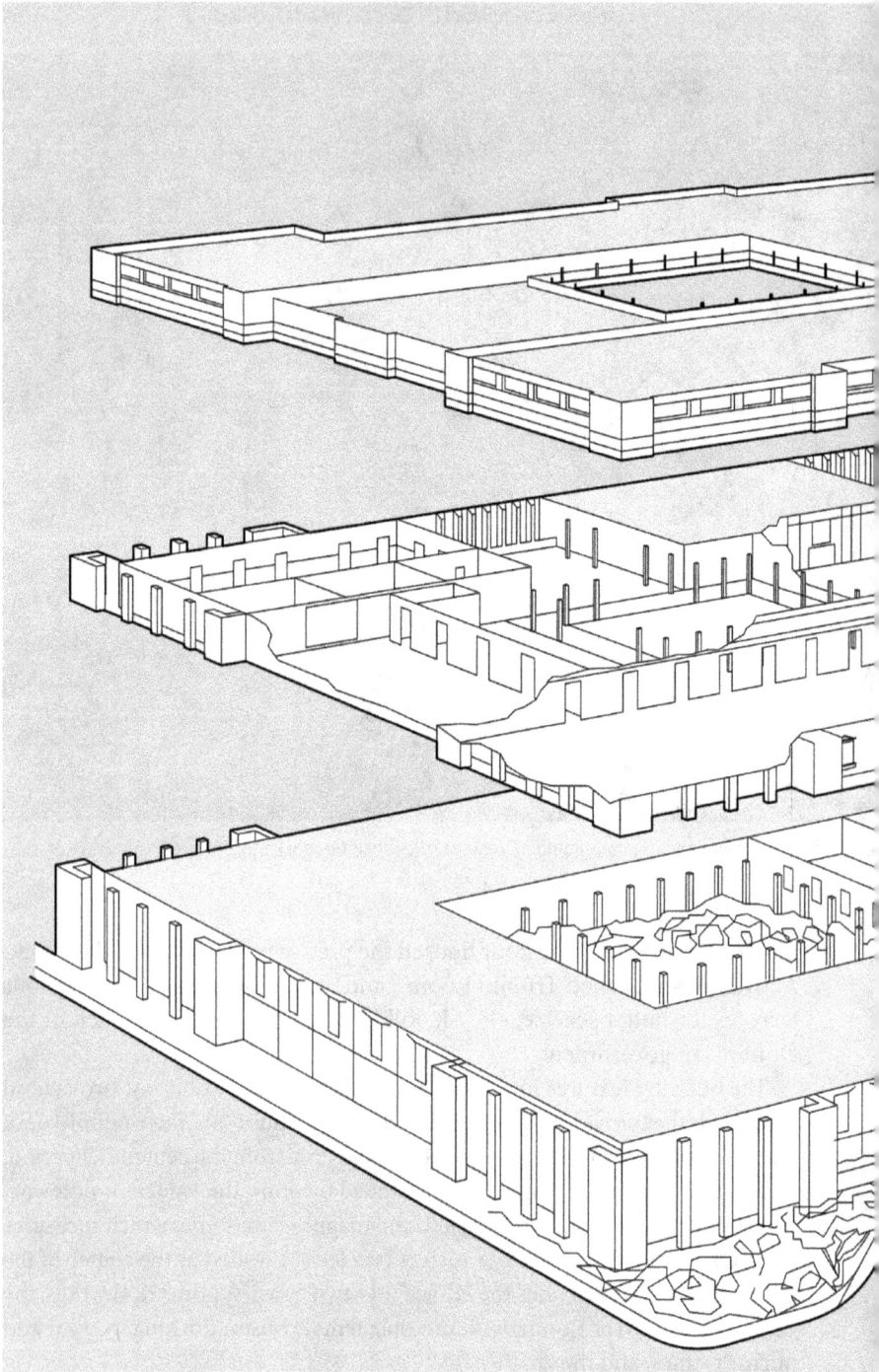

Axonometric rendition, Palacio Nacional, Santo Domingo, Dominican Republic, 1947. AutoCAD rendition by author from existing drawing. From Checo et al., *National Palace*, 134.

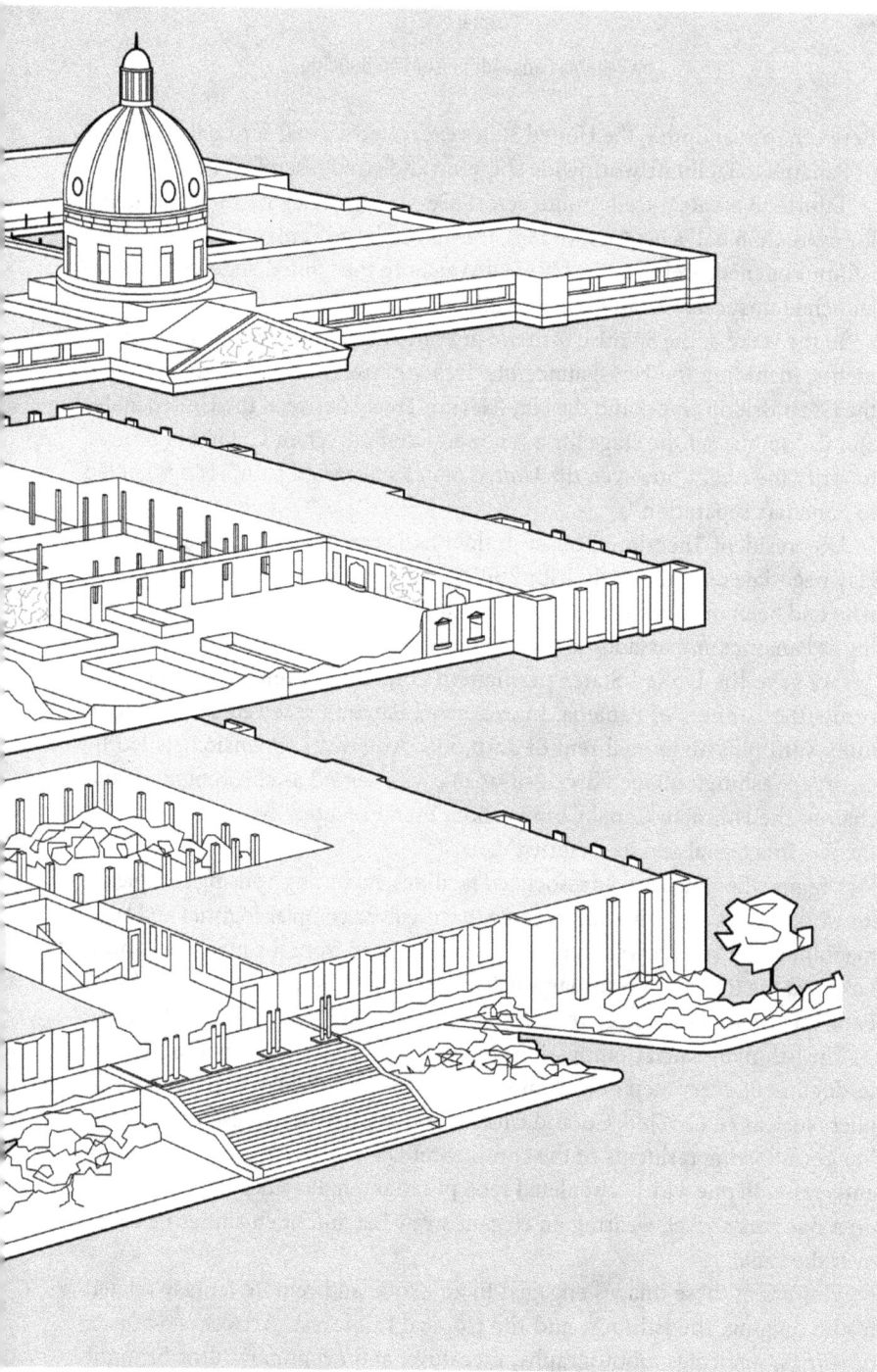

Chapter 2

The Panama Canal Administration Building

Between 1903 and 1914, the United States excavated a canal across the Isthmus of Panama to facilitate worldwide shipping and strengthen US naval power.

Efforts to create a trade route across Central America had been ongoing for more than half a century. In 1855, the first railroad across the Panamanian isthmus opened, and after the US Civil War, both the United States and France launched unsuccessful attempts to build a canal.

In the wake of the Spanish-American War, international political developments, including the Hay-Pauncefote Treaty between the United States and the Great Britain (1901) and the Hay-Herrán Treaty between the United States and Colombia, set the stage for a renewed attempt. When Colombia refused to ratify the treaty, however, the United States supported an uprising that led to Panama's separation.

US president Theodore Roosevelt then had secretary of state John Milton Hay negotiate another treaty with Philippe Bunau-Varilla, a French engineer who had been involved in the earlier canal-building effort and who was serving as Panama's ambassador to the United States. The 1903 Hay–Bunau-Varilla Treaty gave the United States permanent control of a ten-mile-wide zone across the Isthmus of Panama. In exchange, Panama received a $10 million lump sum plus an annual rent of $250,000. American expansionists led by George Washington Goethals (1858–1928), who served as chief engineer and chaired the Isthmian Canal Commission, then executed the construction of the Panama Canal and its facilities.

Digging the canal and its associated facilities, including housing complexes for workers, was a massive undertaking that involved complex logistics and large machinery. Existing towns were flooded and erased from the map, and Gatún Lake—at the time the world's largest artificial body of water—was created. The Panama Canal seal featured the slogan *The Land Divided—The World United*.

The Isthmian Canal Commission employed a constellation of photographers to document every step of the construction process. Professional photographers such as H. C. White Co. and Underwood & Underwood also contributed images, allowing residents of the continental US and elsewhere to follow the enterprise. In one widely circulated 1906 photograph, President Roosevelt sits on a Bucyrus shovel, wearing an elegant straw hat and linen suit as he looks over the canal.

Viewers of these images engaged in an exotic and remote fantasy related to the digging, the isthmus, and the tropical rainforest. Artworks—music, drawings, paintings, photography, literature, and eventually films brought Progressive America closer to the canal, and vice versa. Biographies traced

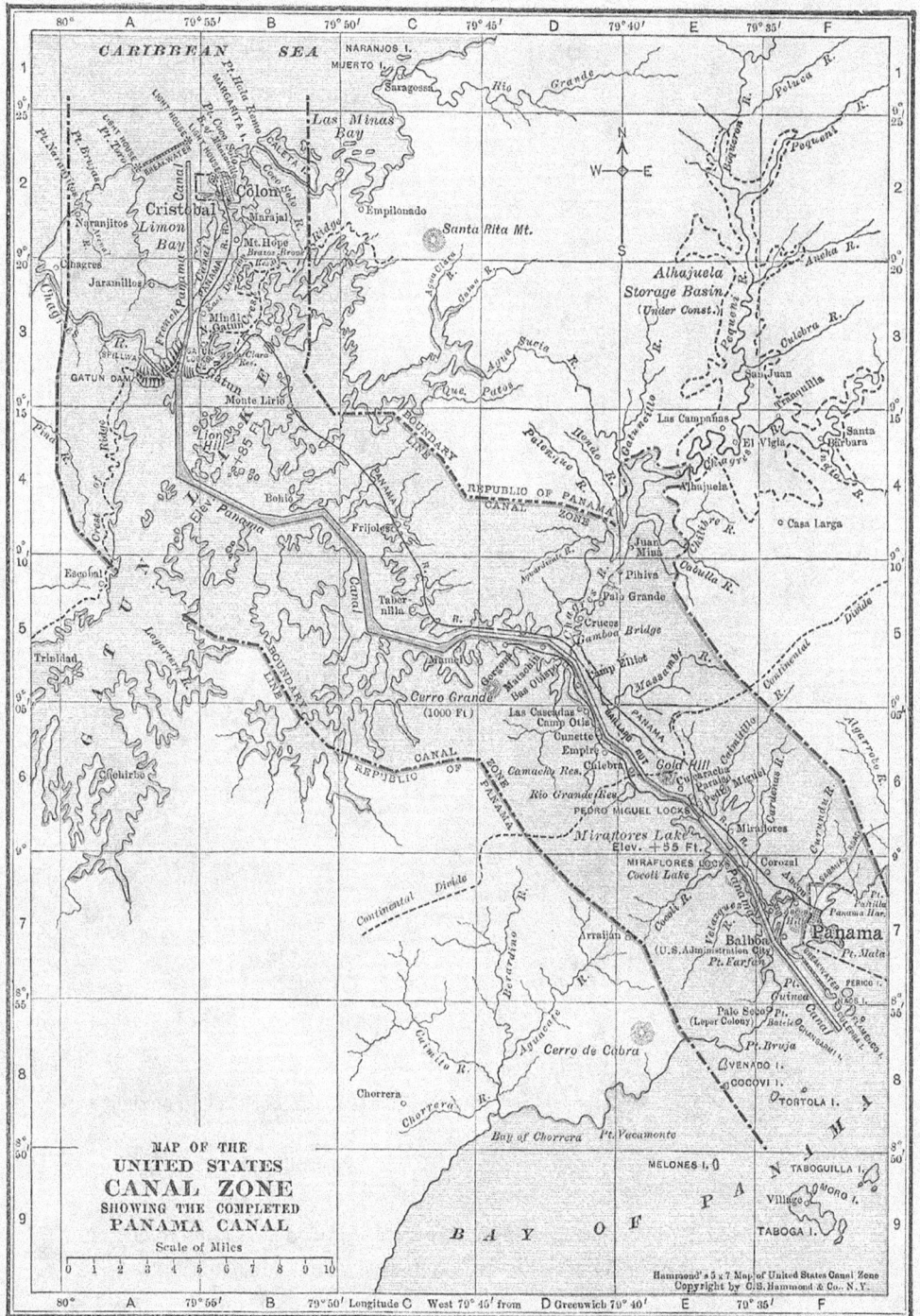

Map of the US Canal Zone, n.d. Courtesy of Special Collections, University of Texas at Arlington Libraries.

Joseph Pennell, *The Gates of Pedro Miguel*, 1912. The Pedro Miguel Lock gates under construction.
Courtesy of the Granger Historical Picture Archive.

the lives of US presidents and engineers involved in constructing the Panama
Canal, while other narratives described its design and construction as well as
the mercantile and shipping activities it would permit. William C. Haskins's
1908 publication, *Canal Zone Pilot: Guide to the Republic of Panama*, was a
significant contribution to this literature. Descriptions of the area's tropical flora

and fauna and sanitation techniques for mosquito control were also popular, as were picturesque depictions of the isthmus and its coastal cities and romantic accounts of pirate attacks during the Spanish Conquest. Poets composed verse about the canal and the isthmus.[6]

In music, Joseph J. Kaiser and William Paris Chambers (1854–1913) composed a march "In Old Panama: Spanish Waltzes," while John Philip Sousa (1854–1932) contributed "Pathfinder of Panama" for the 1915 San Francisco Panama-Pacific International Exposition. The exhibition also featured "Panama Pacific Drag," by composer Leo Edwards (1886–1978), which was included in the Broadway musical *Passing Show of 1915*.[7]

Short documentary films about the canal and isthmus appeared as early as 1907, when both *Colon to Panama Canal Picture* and *Old Market Place, Panama* appeared. In 1914, Hagy Features released a silent documentary, *The Panama Canal*, the portrayed the waterway's construction.

In 1912, American etcher, lithographer, and writer Joseph Pennell (1857–1926) released a portfolio of prints based on the construction of the Panama Canal that captured the massive proportions of its construction process. American impressionist landscape painter Alson Skinner Clark (1876–1949) won a bronze medal at the 1915 Panama-Pacific International Exposition for his work on the struggle between humans and the jungle. In 1913, Norwegian-born American landscape painter Jonas Lie (1880–1940) published a book of art that depicted construction scenes.[8]

The Isthmian Canal Commission retained US landscape painter William van Ingen (1858–1955) to create murals for the Panama Canal Administration Building. Van Ingen was an acolyte of the Hudson River School and a successor of Thomas Cole (1801–48), Asher Brown Durand (1796–1886), and George Inness (1825–94). In 1915, van Ingen installed his paintings in the building's rotunda. He also painted murals and portraits for the Birch Bayh Federal Building and US Courthouse in Indianapolis and the Library of Congress in Washington, DC, among other institutions.

Most of these artworks exalted the United States and its Anglo-Saxon, exceptionalist roots. Minorities were almost completely absent from US art from the Panama Canal era, which either ignored contributions to the construction by Latinos, Afro-Caribbeans, Asians, and Eastern Europeans or portrayed them in secondary roles, performing menial jobs.

Thus, the Canal Zone was depicted as a dull, bidimensional strip that upheld the US military presence in Panama rather than as a diverse, multifaceted region. This depiction was supported by the names of the dozen or so US military bases in the region, which paid homage to such members of the US armed forces as Major General William A. Kobbe, Major Charles H. Howard, Major General Wallace F. Randolph, and General William T. Sherman.[9]

Aerial view, Panama Canal Administration Building and Balboa Townsite. Google Earth.

In planning and constructing the town of Balboa—the capital of the Canal Zone and the site of the Administration Building (see chapter 1)—William Lyman Phillips, Austin Willard Lord, and the US Commission of Fine Arts engaged in efforts to beautify the setting, but the Canal Zone nevertheless developed a conservative, self-destructive entropy. From 1903 to 1977, chain-link fences surrounded the Canal Zone, guarding its military bases and residential neighborhoods. Panamanian citizens could enter the Zona only by permit, whereas fewer restrictions on public access were instituted for the Puerto Rican Capitolio, the Cuban Capitolio, the Dominican Palacio Nacional, and other American Beaux-Arts facilities.

The Panama Canal Administration Building displays École des Beaux-Arts, along with City Beautiful design precepts. Located on the northern mountain of Ancón Hill, the Administration Building evokes a palatine spirit typical of Lord Hewlett & Tallant's works.

Front facade, Panama Canal Administration Building, Balboa, 1914. Photo by author.

Through its semi-astylar formal attributes, the Administration Building at first glance possesses a subdued spirit of place. First, its base, located five feet aboveground, suggests solidity and closeness to the earth. The next level displays Tuscan square columns and two horizontal rows of regular fenestrations. Finally, the third-story wall and the roof, with its dark-red Spanish vitreous tiles and its eaves, emphasize lateral extension.

The building's location atop a knoll and overlooking Balboa evokes the architecture and urban layout of Capitol Hill in Washington, DC. Construction materials include marble mosaics, mahogany, pavonazzo, verde antique, limestone, and Tennessee marble as well as concrete, dark-red clay tiles, edge-grained yellow pine, and quarry tile.

The Administration Building's E-shaped plan and wings evoke a bald eagle ready to take flight. The hidden dome and rotunda allude to US state capitols, highlighting the Canal's exceptionalist character, as well as to the US Government Building at the St. Louis World's Fair. The Administration Building also reflects the influence of supervising architect James Knox Taylor and bears resemblances to the Birch Bayh Federal Building and US Courthouse in Indianapolis and the Frank E. Moss Courthouse in Salt Lake City.

Surrounded by a hall and covered with a suppressed dome, the rotunda emulates the US Capitol and most state capitols, inspiring dignity and grandeur.

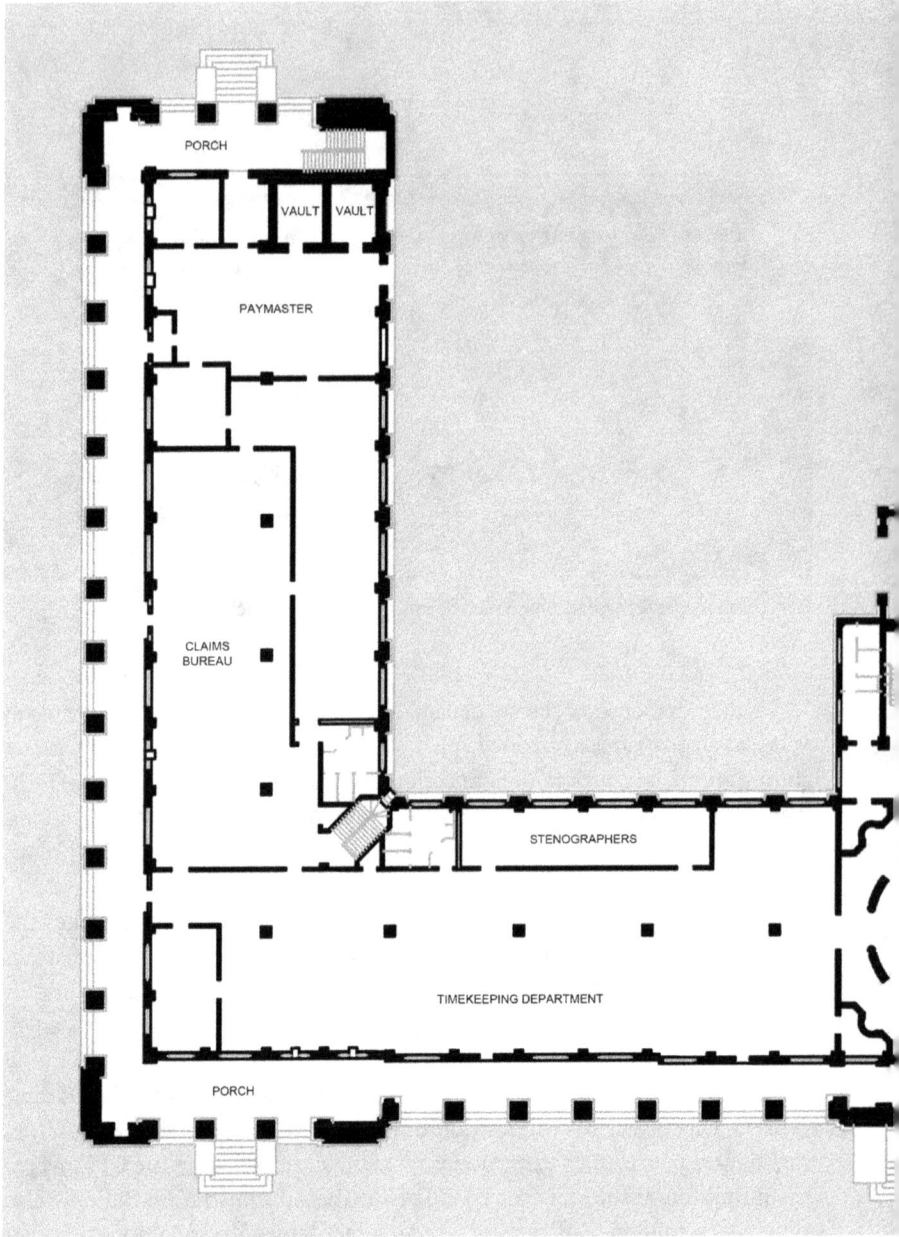

First floor plan, Panama Canal Administration Building, Balboa, 1914. AutoCAD drawing by author from existing drawing. Courtesy of the National Archives, College Park, Maryland.

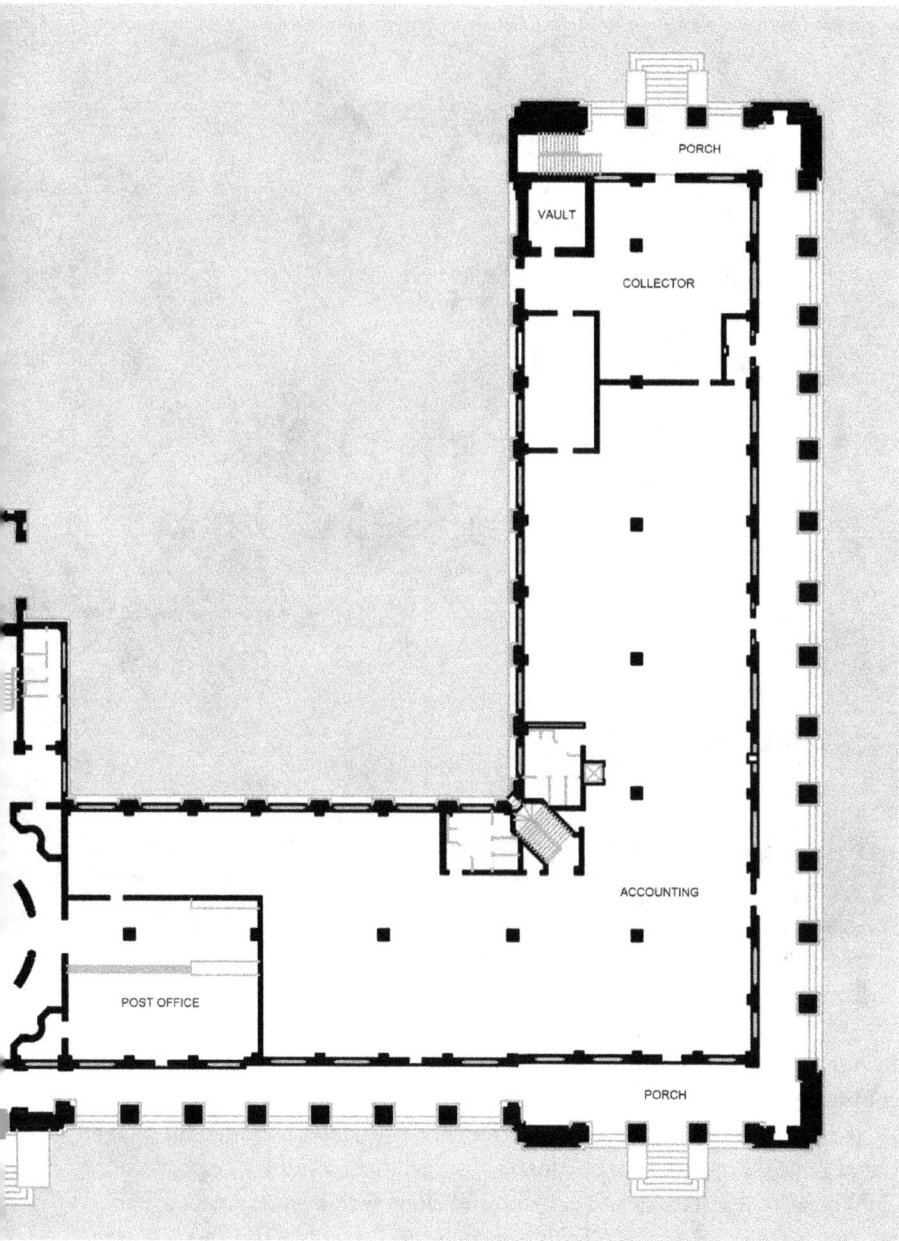

PORCH

VAULT

COLLECTOR

ACCOUNTING

POST OFFICE

PORCH

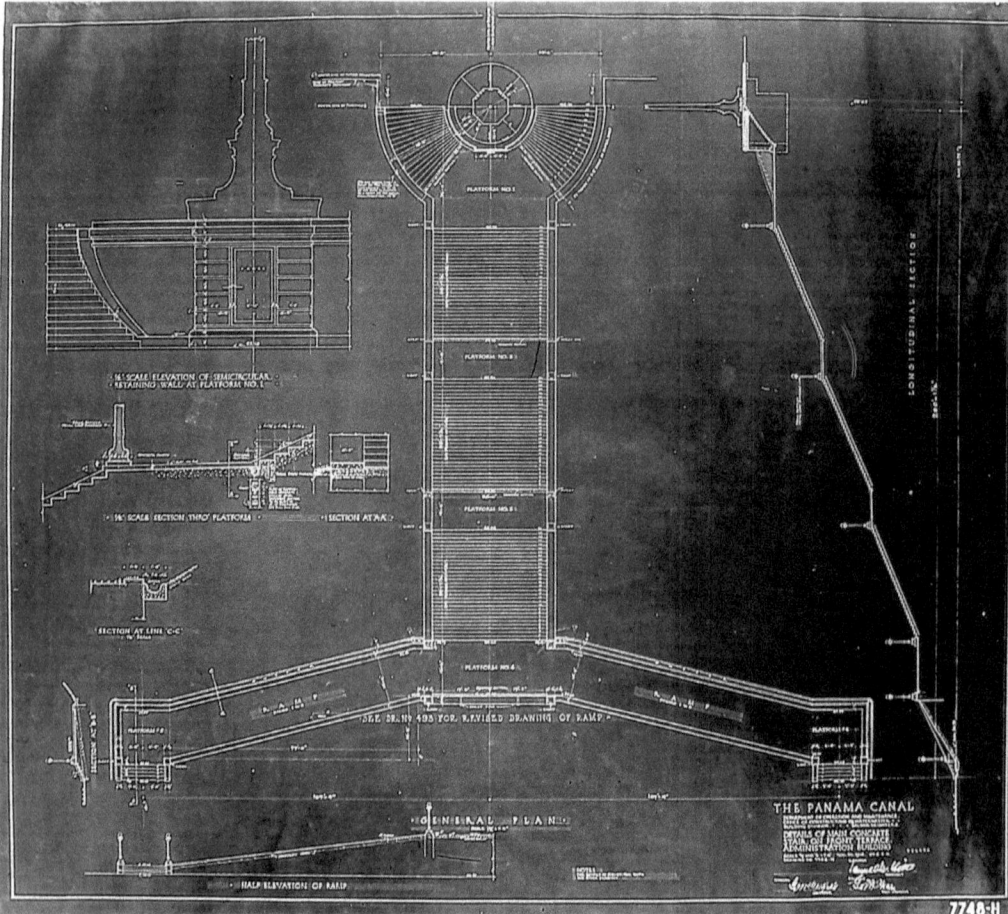

Ramps and front escalade (drawing), Panama Canal Administration Building, Balboa, 1914. Courtesy of the National Archives, College Park, Maryland.

At one time, the building housed the offices of the Canal Zone governor; it continues to provide office space for the canal administration.

The layout for the new urban settlement of Balboa included all of the Canal Zone's administrative and mercantile facilities (commissary, post office, clubhouse, police station, and courthouse) along with a *prado* (main avenue) offering a scenic view of the Pacific entrance to the canal. The area featured precast balustrades, terraces, concrete and asphalt street paving, and 15,500 trees and plants as well as lighting and sewage.

At an urban design level, the Administration Building's front ramps and escalades evoke the presence of an open, outdoor *salle des pas-perdus* that connects

Ramp and front escalade (view), Panama Canal Administration Building, Balboa, 1914. Photo by author.

the precinct to its surroundings. They still provide stages for political, artistic, and historical events, with crowds gathering on the hillside for notable events.

Although the Isthmian Canal Commission retained Austin Willard Lord as the building's architect, Samuel Hitt and Mario Schiavoni (b. 1883) finished the project. Schiavoni worked at Graham, Anderson, Probst & White (successor to D. H. Burnham & Co.). He completed his studies at the École des Beaux-Arts in 1910.

It remains an open question whether the Canal Zone made the Administration Building a Latin American structure, or another iteration of an American colony overseas.

Charles Follen McKim, ca. 1890–1909. Courtesy of the Prints and Photographs Division, Library of Congress. L-11735, LC-DIG-ds-04713, LC-USZ62-58760.

CHAPTER 3

RELEVANT DESIGNERS FROM THE TARSNEY ACT ERA

This chapter highlights the work of late nineteenth-century American architects trained in the Beaux-Arts tradition who produced magnificent examples of federal architecture in the United States and abroad. While some of their designs remained loyal to the Beaux-Arts tradition, others showed more modern influences.

Charles Follen McKim (1847-1909): Founding Member of McKim, Mead & White

McKim became interested in architecture while studying mining engineering at Harvard's Lawrence Scientific School. Switching fields, he went to Paris, studied at the Atelier Daumet of the École des Beaux-Arts, and traveled across Europe. Back in the United States, he worked at Gambrill & Richardson as a draftsperson.

McKim joined with William R. Mead to found an architectural firm in 1872, adding William Bigelow as a partner six years later. Shortly thereafter, Stanford White superseded Bigelow, resulting in the creation of McKim, Mead & White.

Following his training at the École, McKim developed a keen interest in neoclassicism. He also introduced the Italian Renaissance and Romanesque design alternatives in his work. Notable works in McKim, Mead & White's extensive portfolio include the Boston Public Library (1895), the Low Memorial

Daniel Hudson Burnham, ca. 1880. Courtesy of the Archives of American Art, Smithsonian Institution.

Library at New York's Columbia University (1895), and the Rhode Island State-house in Providence (1904). Among the well-known architects who started their careers under McKim's tutelage are Thomas Moore Kellogg, Cass Gilbert, Henry Bacon (who designed the Lincoln Memorial in Washington, DC), and Austin Willard Lord.

McKim received honorary degrees from Harvard, Columbia, and Princeton Universities and became a Fellow of the American Institute of Architects. McKim received Gold Medals from the Royal Institute of British Architects in 1903 and from the American Institute of Architects in 1909. He was a founder and early president of the American Academy in Rome.

Daniel Hudson Burnham (1846-1912):
First Chair of the US Commission of Fine Arts

Burnham was a notable architect and city planner with offices in Chicago. He began his career as an apprentice for William LeBaron Jenney (1832–1907) and worked as a draftsperson at Carter, Drake & Wight, where he met John Wellborn Root (1850–91). In 1873, he and Root became partners in the Chicago

James Knox Taylor, 1897. From *Inland Architect and News Record* 30 (November 1897): 37.

firm of Burnham & Root, taking advantage of the commissions available as a result of rebuilding efforts in the wake of the 1871 Great Fire.

For the 1893 World's Columbian Exposition, Root served as a consulting architect and Burnham was construction chief; the firm of F. L. Olmsted served as landscape architects. When Root died suddenly of pneumonia, Burnham assumed his partner's architectural responsibilities.

In 1901, Burnham became chair of the Senate Park Commission, and in 1910, he chaired the US Commission of Fine Arts.

James Knox Taylor (1857–1929): Supervising Architect

James Knox Taylor served as the Treasury Department's supervising architect between 1897 and 1912. He had previously practiced as an architect in Philadelphia and Washington, DC, with one of his classmates at the Massachusetts Institute of Technology, Amos J. Boyden (1853–1903). He also worked for McKim, Mead & White as well as for Cass Gilbert in Charles Haight's (1841–1917) and Bruce Price's (1845–1903) offices. After retiring as supervising architect, Taylor continued his architectural practice in Boston.

INTERNATIONAL BUREAU OF THE AMERICAN REPUBLICS BUILDING.
ALBERT KELSEY & PAUL P. CRET, ARCHITECTS.

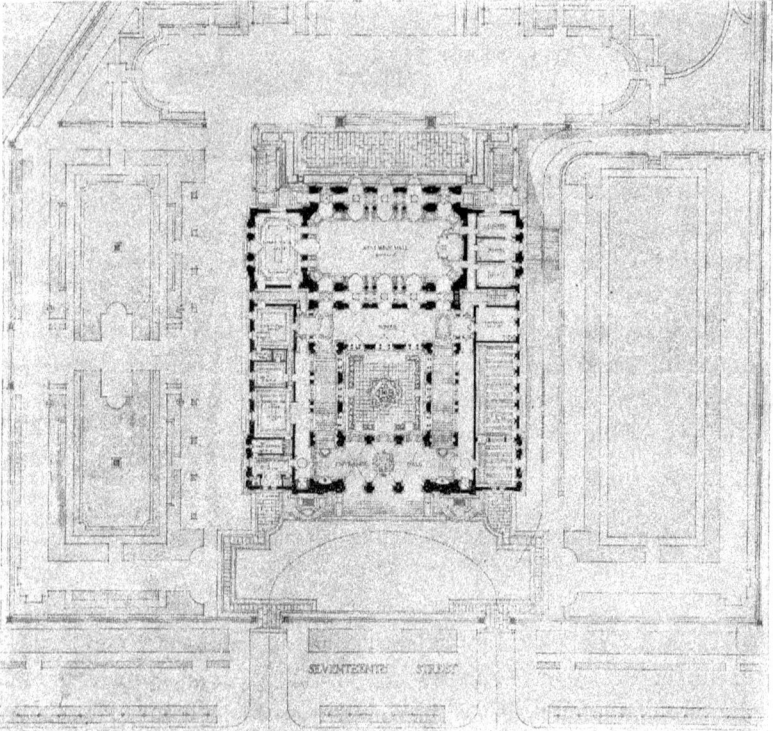

INTERNATIONAL BUREAU OF THE AMERICAN REPUBLICS BUILDING.
ALBERT KELSEY & PAUL P. CRET, ARCHITECTS.

Paul Philippe Cret, front facade and first floor plan, Pan American Union Building, Washington, DC, 1907. Courtesy of the Philadelphia Architects and Buildings Project.

Paul Philippe Cret, 1910. Paul Philippe Cret Collection, Architectural Archives, University of Pennsylvania.

Paul Philippe Cret, Pan American Union Building, Washington, DC, 2018. Photo by author.

Paul Philippe Cret (1876-1945): Architect of the Pan American Union Building

French architect Paul Philippe Cret was a precursor of works showcasing American exceptionalism in US foreign lands. In 1903, after studying under Jean-Louis Pascal at the École des Beaux-Arts, Cret arrived in the United States to teach architectural history at the University of Pennsylvania. He opened an architectural partnership with Albert Kelsey (1870–1950), and in 1907, a

Paul Philippe Cret, Pan American Union Building, Washington, DC, 1907, front facade and first floor plan. Courtesy of the Philadelphia Architects and Buildings Project.

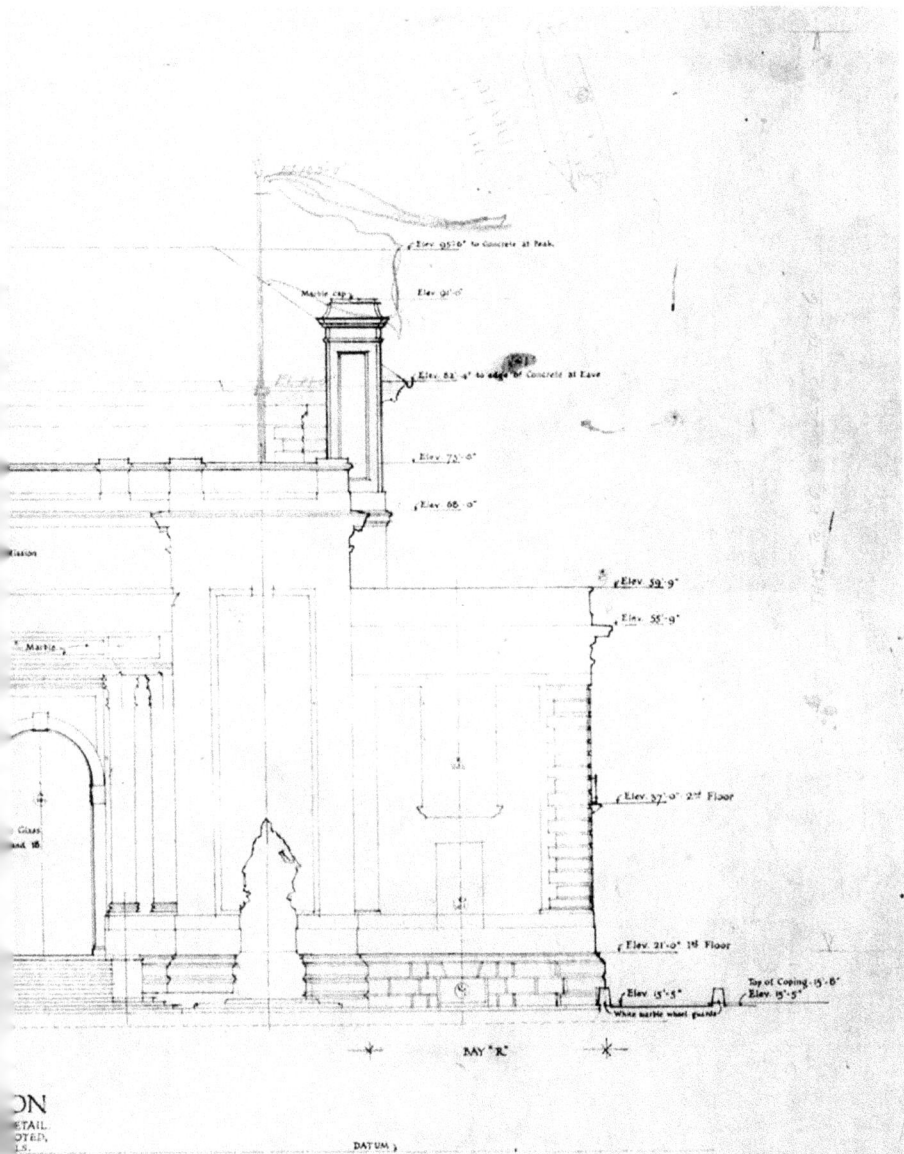

Elev. 95'-6" to Concrete at Peak.

Elev. 91'-6"

Marble cap.

Elev. 83'-4" to edge of Concrete at Eave

Elev. 75'-0"

Elev. 68'-0"

Elev. 59'-9"

Elev. 55'-9"

Marble

Glass
and 18.

Elev. 37'-0" 2nd Floor

Elev. 21'-0" 1st Floor

Elev. 15'-5"

Top of Coping. 15'-6"
Elev. 15'-5"

White marble wheel guards

BAY "R"

DATUM

RICAN · REPVBLICS
C
ET
)
ER

COM · 238 · SHEET · NO · 7
SCALE · ⅛ INCH · 1 FOOT
DATE · FEBRUARY 5 1906

Gertrude Vanderbilt Whitney, ca. 1910.
Courtesy of the Archives of American Art,
Smithsonian Institution.

Gertrude Vanderbilt Whitney, sketch of the Aztec Fountain, Pan American Union Building, 1912. Paul
Philippe Cret Collection, Architectural Archives, University of Pennsylvania.

Gertrude Vanderbilt Whitney, Aztec Fountain, Pan American Union Building, 1912. Photo by author.

jury that included Charles Follen McKim, Austin Willard Lord, and Henry Hornbostel (1867–1961) selected the firm to design the Pan American Union Building in Washington, DC.

In keeping with his academic training, Cret created works that followed the rhythm and scale of classical canons, formally articulating the language of a Renaissance Roman palazzo. This approach is exemplified by the Indianapolis Central Library (1917), the Detroit Institute of Arts (1923–27), and the Marriner S. Eccles Federal Reserve Board Building in Washington, DC (1937).

Cret's architectural designs reveal a mélange of both assimilative and associative overtones. Cret's École des Beaux-Arts training led him to use balance and

Paul Philippe Cret, Folger Shakespeare Library, Washington, DC, 2018. Photo by author.

symmetry in his friezes, capitals, bases, and balustrades, but he also incorporated traditional classicist elements, creating a sense of associative exceptionalism or Americanization. This Americanization is evident in the Aztec Fountain in the central courtyard of the Pan American Union Building, which was sculpted in 1912 by Gertrude Vanderbilt Whitney (1875–1942). Whitney had studied at the Art Students League of New York and in Paris, and she went on to become not only a noted sculptor but also a patron of the arts.

In 1915, Whitney won an award at the Panama-Pacific International Exposition for her Fountain of El Dorado. Other works included the Titanic Memorial (1914–31) in Washington, DC and the Washington Heights War Memorial (1921) and Peter Stuyvesant Monument (1936–39), both in New York. She founded the Whitney Museum of American Art and was a contributor to the Whitney Wing of the American Museum of Natural History.

The Pan American Union Building's entrance is flanked by two statues allegorizing South and North America, the work of Isidore Konti (1862–1938) and Gutzon Borglum (1867–1941).

Konti contributed sculptures for a variety of US fairs, including the 1893 World's Columbian Exposition in Chicago. Borglum is widely known for his carvings of the US presidents on Mount Rushmore as well as his possible affiliation with the Ku Klux Klan. Cret distanced himself from contemporary Washington architects such as Marion Sims Wyeth (1889–1982) and George Oakley Totten Jr. (1866–1939) by introducing vernacular touches in his Beaux-

Paul Philippe Cret, Pan American Union Building, Washington, DC, 1907.

Arts designs. In addition to incorporating decorative artifacts by artists such as Whitney who were inspired by indigenous works, Cret alluded to Meso-american ornamentation in exterior moldings and light fixtures in his Pan American Union Building.

The Pan American Union Building's Aztec Courtyard (Patio Azteca) became one of its signature features. According to Elizabeth Greenwell Grossman, Kelsey visited Mexico to familiarize himself with pre-Columbian motifs for the building's decoration.[1] In contrast, for the interior decoration of Wyeth's MacVeagh Mansion, the Embassy of Mexico retained a local artist, Roberto Cueva Del Rio (1908–88), to paint its murals between 1933 and 1941, several years after the building opened to the public.

Thus, Cret became a proponent of exceptionalist civic architecture in the Americas through his formal approaches, opening new ground for US government Beaux-Arts architecture in the Western Hemisphere.

Bertram Grosvenor Goodhue (1869–1924): Architect of the Panama-California Exposition

Two California World's Fairs celebrated the opening of the Panama Canal and its massive impact on maritime infrastructure worldwide: the Panama-Pacific International Exposition in San Francisco in 1915, and the Panama-California

Bertram Grosvenor Goodhue, n.d. Courtesy of the San Diego Historical Society.

Bertram Grosvenor Goodhue, Washington Hotel, Colón, Panama, 1913. Courtesy of the Library of Congress Prints and Photographs Division, Washington, DC, National Capital Planning Commission.

Exposition in San Diego from 1915 to 1917. The galleries and exhibits at the two fairs exalted what was then heralded as the Eighth Wonder of the World.

The Panama-Pacific International Exposition also signaled San Francisco's resurgence after the earthquake and fire of 1906. The exposition's centerpiece, the Tower of Jewels, was covered with 100,000 cut-glass "Novagems" that sparkled in the sunshine by day and when hit by the beams of searchlights at night. With the exception of the Palace of Fine Arts, by Bernard Maybeck (1862–1957), however, all of the structures built for the fair were abandoned and demolished.

The Panama-California Exposition brought significant recognition to San Diego. The fair was held on 1,200 acres in what is now Balboa Park and became widely known for its landscape and horticulture projects. Architects Bertram Grosvenor Goodhue (1869–1924) and Carleton Winslow (1876–1946) adopted a Spanish Colonial Revival design, a hybrid of Baroque Churrigueresque and Renaissance Plateresque styles.

Goodhue had already become a renowned architect after apprenticing at Renwick, Aspinwall & Russell in New York City between 1884 and 1991. He then became the principal of Cram, Goodhue and Ferguson in Boston. In 1925, the American Institute of Architects awarded him its Gold Medal.

Goodhue designed multiple landmarks, among them the Washington Hotel in Colón, Panama (1913); the Nebraska State Capitol in Lincoln (1924); and the Los Angeles Central Library (1926; finished by Winslow after Goodhue's

Jean-Claude Nicolas Forestier, n.d.
https://commons.wikimedia.org/
wiki/File:JCN-Forestier.jpg.

death). He also designed an administration building for the Panama-California Exposition complex.

Running parallel to the Panama-Pacific International Exposition in San Francisco was a more minor festival by the same name in Panama City, Panama. The fair commemorated not only the waterway but the four hundredth anniversary of Vasco Núñez de Balboa's 1513 crossing of the isthmus. Belisario Porras Plaza (formerly Cervantes Plaza) in the La Exposición neighborhood served as a stage for two exhibits between Avenida Perú and Calle 33A. Those facilities, which reflect the influences of the City Beautiful movement, now serve as offices for Panama's governor and as the Spanish Embassy.

Jean-Claude Nicolas Forestier (1861–1930): A French Landscape Architect in Havana

Surrounding the Cuban Capitolio, French landscape architect Jean-Claude Nicolas Forestier created a magnificent Beaux-Arts master plan incorporating an array of lampposts, royal palm trees, pathways, and *tapis verts*. Forestier received his training with Jean Charles Alphand (1817–1891), an engineer who

Frederick Law Olmsted, 1893. Courtesy
of the US Department of the Interior,
National Park Service, Frederick Law
Olmsted National Historic Site.

served as director of public works in Paris and created the city's park system. In Paris, Forestier designed an arboretum at Vincennes and gardens for the Champ-de-Mars below the Eiffel Tower.

In 1925, Forestier moved to Havana and collaborated with local architects on a master plan for the city. He designed gardens for the Casa de Juan Pedro Baró (1927), the Plaza de la Fraternidad Americana (1928), the Paseo del Prado (1929), and the grand staircase of the University of Havana. He also planned urban improvements in Buenos Aires, Argentina, and in Spain, where he designed Seville's Maria Luisa Park and the gardens of Ronda's Casa del Rey Moro. His writings include *Jardins: Carnet de plans et de croquis* (1908), and *Grandes villes et systèmes de parcs* (1908).

Frederick Law Olmsted (1822–1903):
Insights from a Landscapist Standpoint

American landscape architect, journalist, social critic, and public administrator Frederick Law Olmsted joined with Calvert Vaux (1824–95) to found Olmsted, Vaux & Co. in 1865. The firm went on to complete hundreds of landscape projects, perhaps most notably New York's Central Park and San Francisco's Golden Gate Park. According to Lewis Mumford, "If, as Olmsted pointed out, the movement towards urban parks was almost an instinctive one throughout Western Civilization, after the middle of the nineteenth century, in reaction against the depression and misery of the industrial city, Olmsted gave it a rationale."[2]

One of the highlights of Olmsted's career was his landscape design for the 1893 Columbian Exposition in Chicago. In the words of Charles Moore,

> The plat contemplated an architectural court, similar to the one at the Paris Exposition. This court should enclose a body of water and should serve as a dignified and impressive entrance hall to the Exposition. There was a formal canal leading northward from the court to a series of broader waters of a lagoon character, by which nearly the entire site would be penetrated, so that the principal buildings would have a water as well as a land frontage and would be approachable by boat. Also, it was decided that near the middle of the lagoon system there should be an island fifteen acres in area, in which would be clusters of the largest trees growing upon the site; that this island should be free from conspicuous buildings and that it should have a generally secluded, natural, sylvan aspect.[3]

Frederick Law Olmsted Jr. (1870-1957): Founding Member of the US Commission of Fine Arts

Frederick Law Olmsted Jr. followed in his father's footsteps, becoming an immensely successful landscape architect. In 1910, the younger Olmsted became a founding member of the US Commission of Fine Arts, which was active in designing the Panama Canal Administration Building and in laying out the town of Balboa. The commission addressed the artistic character of the Panama Canal and its complementary structures.

Olmsted and sculptor Daniel Chester French (1850–1931) visited the isthmus in 1912 to report on the project's progress. The canal's chief engineer, George Washington Goethals, adopted their recommendations, which included a sparing use of ornamentation in the design and construction of the Administration Building and a focus on the waterway's practical and mercantile functions. The commission recentered Balboa's layout around an axis that extended from the Administration Building's rotunda to the top of Sosa Hill. The new design reoriented the Administration Building and increased its visibility from the Pacific entrance to the canal.

Frederick Law Olmsted Jr., n.d. Courtesy of the US Department of the Interior, National Park Service, Frederick Law Olmsted National Historic Site.

The US Commission of Fine Arts also endorsed commemorative murals for the rotunda and a memorial in front of the building, though the Goethals Monument, which followed Cret's preliminary design from 1939, did not open until 1954.

Olmsted and the Commission of Fine Arts provided the city of Balboa with a unified vision of its architecture and urban design—and its corporate branding.

William Lyman Phillips, n.d. Courtesy of the
Fairchild Tropical Botanic Garden.

William Lyman Phillips (1885-1966):
Landscape Architect for the Town of Balboa

In 1908, William Lyman Phillips received a landscape architecture degree from at
Harvard University, where he studied under Frederick Law Olmsted Jr. Phillips
joined the Olmsted Brothers firm in 1911 and started working on government
projects in the United States and abroad two years later. At Camp Las Casas
in San Juan, Puerto Rico, he worked in the US Army's Quartermaster's Corps
Construction Division.

In 1913, the Isthmian Canal Commission retained Phillips as a landscape
architect for the town of Balboa.

> He cut a long straight line—a wide avenue, or prado, with double roadways on
> either side and central parking—from the administration building on Ancon
> directly across to the large elliptical Balboa Plaza below it at the foot of Sosa Hill,
> ending at the clubhouse square, which he designed, on the old La Boca road. He
> designated the prado the "formal part of our town," outlined with royal palms,
> with a long driveway entrance, also palm-lined, "a setting for the important, if not
> architecturally charming, existing Administration building. . . . I am not fond of
> this feather duster tree [the royal palm], but the chairman is; he thinks it is the
> finest tree that grows . . . [so] I intend to use it [freely]."[4]

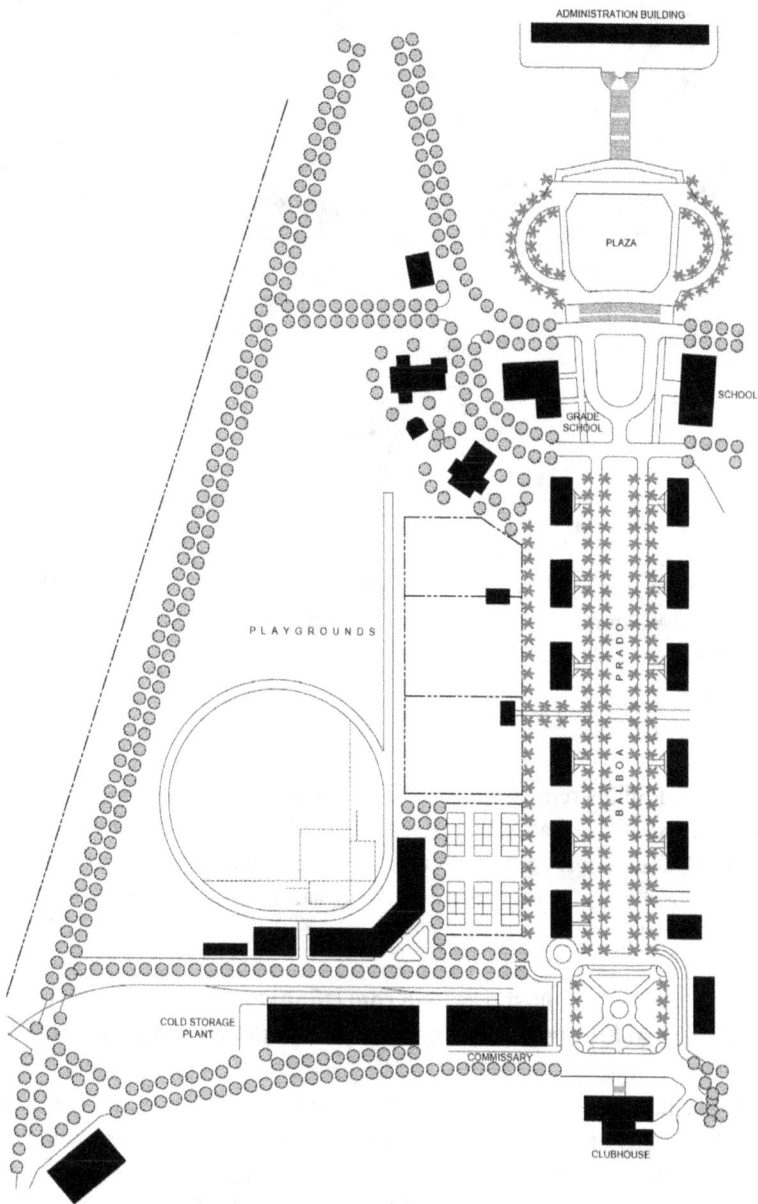

William Lyman Phillips, permanent grounds for the town of Balboa, Panama, 1913–14. AutoCAD Drawing by author from existing drawing. Courtesy of the George A. Smathers Libraries, Digital Collections, University of Florida.

From the William Lyman Phillips Photograph Collection, ca. 1920s–40s. Courtesy of the Archives of American Gardens, Smithsonian Institution.

In 1925, Phillips returned to Olmsted Brothers, where his projects involved assignments with the National Park Service, the Civilian Conservation Corps, and Florida's Dade County Parks and Recreation Department. The Fairchild Tropical Botanic Garden in Coral Gables, Florida, became one of his signature designs.

Austin Willard Lord (1860–1922):
Original Architect of the Panama Canal Administration Building

Austin Willard Lord was well connected to the professional architectural elite. Born in Rolling Stone, Minnesota, Lord received his architectural training at the Massachusetts Institute of Technology, receiving his degree in 1884. He obtained a Rotch Traveling Scholarship in 1887 and studied at the Paris ateliers of Honoré Daumet and Charles Girault between 1889 and 1890.

Lord briefly joined the firm of McKim, Mead & White and was selected by Charles Follen McKim as the first director of the American Academy in Rome. He and James Monroe Hewlett (1868–1941) established late

Austin Willard Lord, ca. 1916. From *The Brickbuilder* 25, no. 1 (January 1916): 23.

nineteenth-century practice in New York City, Lord, Hewlett and Tallant, that met with great success. Hewlett had also worked for McKim, Mead & White and acted as director of the academy. Many of Lord, Hewlett and Tallant's commissions involved luxurious residences in New Jersey. With Albert Kelsey of Cret and Kelsey, Lord worked on the plan for the city of Columbus, Ohio (1908).

By the time of the Administration Building's design and construction, Lord had become a renowned architect and painter. In addition, he served as head of the Department of Architecture at Columbia University, where he endorsed the Beaux-Arts academic tradition. That stylistic influence as well as the City Beautiful movement conditioned Lord's designs for the Panama Canal Administration Building and the Prado. His controlled symmetry and restrained ostentation helped to convey a branded mercantile and maritime image to the world.

An involvement of Lord's architectural partners into his buildings and designs is unknown. Hewlett, for example, neither designed nor painted the murals in the Administration Building, but as an architect, muralist, and set designer, he may have played a role in the decision process that led to their creation. Hewlett painted murals for the Willard Straight Memorial at Cornell University and the Elihu Root Memorial in Washington, DC. He served as president of the Architectural League of New York and the Society of Mural Painters and as vice

Masonic Temple, Clermont Avenue and Lafayette Avenue, Brooklyn, New York, 1909. Photo by George P. Hall & Son. George P. Hall & Son Photograph Collection, PR 024. nyhs_PR024_b-19_ f-172_002-01. Photograph © New-York Historical Society.

president of the American Institute of Architects, director of the Fontainebleau School in Paris, and resident director of the American Academy in Rome.

The third partner in Lord and Hewlett's firm, Hugh Tallant (1869–1952), had previously worked for Herts & Tallant, known for designs of such New York City theaters as the New Amsterdam, the Fulton, the Gaiety, and the Liberty. One of Herts & Tallant's works is Coram Library (1902) at Bates College in Maine. Its rectangular front facade, adorned with neoclassical columns, evokes both the dramatic effects and the institutional, bureaucratic character of the Administration Building on a more modest scale.

Lord & Hewlett, Tollemache House. Mendham, New Jersey, 1894–95. Courtesy of John K. Turpin, W. Barry Thomson, and David Gruol.

Lord & Hewlett, Greystock Manor, Mendham, New Jersey, 1915. Courtesy of John K. Turpin, W. Barry Thomson, and Billy Prouty.

Lord & Hewlett, Hunt/Ruxcroft House, Pleasant Valley, New Jersey, 1900. Courtesy of John K. Turpin and W. Barry Thomson.

The Lord & Hewlett–designed Woodmere Farms/Tollemache House in Mendham, New Jersey, (1894–95) shows an austere, Classical Revival style. This two-story residence follows a rectangular plan. In the middle of Tollemache's front facade, a two-story portico with four white Ionic columns supports an entablature and a triangular pediment similar to what might be found in a small classical temple. Symmetrical wings are typical of Lord, Hewlett & Tallant designs.

The house's name came from the Norman spelling of the name of the owner, Edward Talmage. In 1926, he partially demolished the structure to construct a new residence on the 400-acre estate.

Greystock Manor, a two-story brick house in the hills outside Mendham, was designed by Lord & Hewlett in 1915. This residence exudes an ethereal spirit of timelessness through its elongated, symmetrical, and balanced proportions.

The Hunt/Ruxcroft House follows the style of an old Normandy farmhouse. Located on Bernardsville Mountain in Pleasant Valley, New Jersey, it was built at the turn of the twentieth century for Thomas Hunt, a Yale-educated attorney who served as secretary of the navy under President James A. Garfield and as a minister to Russia under President Chester A. Arthur.

Situated on approximately seventy acres, Ruxcroft was located on top of a hill, with beautiful views of Pleasant Valley and its surroundings and with two wings set at a forty-five-degree angle from each other: one for the family and another for the servants. Its main feature was an octagonal stair tower with

Cass Gilbert, 1905. Courtesy
of the Prints and Photographs
Division, Library of Congress.
LC-H25-33974-H [P&P], LC-DIG-
hec-18023.

a water storage tank on the roof. The house was demolished in the late 1950s and its stone reused to construct the rectory for the Episcopal Church of St. John on the Mountain.

Cass Gilbert (1859–1934) and the US Commission of Fine Arts

Cass Gilbert was an immensely influential, well-connected, and successful architect. After studying for a year at the Massachusetts Institute of Technology, where he roomed with James Knox Taylor, Gilbert spent nearly a year in Europe. After working at McKim, Mead & White, he relocated to Minneapolis, where he and Taylor formed a practice, Gilbert & Taylor. A decade later, Gilbert moved to New York City. He became a fellow of the American Institute of Architects in 1889 and served as its president in 1908–9. He also became president of the Architectural League of New York (1913–14) and was a member of the Senate Park Commission, where he contributed to the McMillan Plan, and of the US Commission of Fine Arts.

Informed by his espousal of Beaux-Arts principles, Gilbert's design guidelines featured two major exceptionalist concepts, order and system, that became staples of US government architecture overseas. For Gilbert,

order and system, a high state of organization, are elemental conditions of government. These conditions pervade all phases of the service. The relation of
departments is not fortuitous, but definite, organic, and in a sense mechanical.
The city is part of the mechanism. The departmental buildings, the Capitol, the
White House, are details of this machinery. Their excuse for existing is that they
are so. The arrangement of this machinery should not be left to whim, chance, or
to the incident of temporal control. The founders of the Government recognized
this, and Washington himself was foremost in putting it into effect. It needs no
argument: it is self-evident when stated. Nor does the acceptance of such conditions imply naked utilitarianism. On the contrary, they are the first elements in
any grand scheme.[5]

Gilbert's works ranged from skyscrapers (Woolworth Building, New York,
1913) to state capitols (Minnesota, 1905; Arkansas, 1915; and West Virginia,
1925) to art museums (St. Louis, 1904; Allen Memorial, Oberlin, Ohio, 1917)
and educational projects (Battle Hall, the University of Texas at Austin, 1911).
Even after the Tarsney Act scandal, Gilbert continued to receive commissions.

CONCLUSIONS

At the turn of the twentieth century, American exceptionalism proselytized US public Beaux-Arts architecture and urban design, exerting its power over audiences' tastes and imprinting a civic figurative language onto US territories and occupied land. This dogmatic, noninclusive aesthetics became a geopolitical banner for Progressive America. From a broader perspective, the history of American architecture was reinvented through the advent of new technologies (elevators, electricity), construction materials (steel, reinforced concrete), equipment (steam-powered machinery), and real estate demands (skyscrapers). In addition, the era's world's fairs and spectacles inspired the design and construction of new Beaux-Arts government works that consolidated a nationalistic age of architectural aesthetics by glorifying foreign lands via the construction of ephemeral, quasi-celestial "white cities" and thus creating a sense of entitlement within Progressive America.

Many of these structures became prototypes for state, county, and city facilities in the United States and its possessions. Because the École des Beaux-Arts had played such a significant role in training American architects in the classical canon and precepts, Beaux-Arts precepts were translated into formal standards and patterns that conveyed a strong, message of US leadership around the world. Eventually, both the modern movement and the International Style introduced a tradition of the new, obliterating the Beaux-Arts tradition and the scorned Tarsney Act.

Architects, contractors, and tradespersons showed off their expertise thus shaping the collective spatial memory of Progressive America both on the mainland and abroad. This architecture still engages Americans and others around the world, making the Progressive past a legacy for future generations.

GUY DEBORD (1931-1994) AND HIS EXCEPTIONALIST SPECTACLE

For Guy Debord, author of *The Society of the Spectacle*, concrete phenomena such as facilities constructed for world's fairs, the Panama Canal Administration Building, the Puerto Rican Capitolio, the Cuban Capitolio, and the Dominican Palacio Nacional are nothing but spectacles, mediated by images:

> Since the spectacle's job is to cause a world that is no longer directly perceptible to be seen via different specialized mediations, it is inevitable that it should elevate the human sense of sight to the special place once occupied by touch; the most abstract of the senses, and the most easily deceived, sight is naturally the most readily adaptable to present-day society's generalized abstraction. . . . The spectacle is by definition immune from human activity, inaccessible to any projected review or correction. It is the opposite of dialogue.[1]

As a product of a hollow sign system, or rift, a spectacle manifests as enormous positivity: everything that appears is good; whatever is good will appear. Not merely innocuous, these spectacles are promoted and manipulated by a dominant production system. Through hierarchical visual categories and blurred individual acceptances, the spectacle becomes the main component of Western society.

Debord's explanations of the world, or "theses," evidence a detailed yet restrained hostility toward the status quo. His descriptions are ardent and sharp, but he is respectful and sincere to his readers. Both *spectacle* and *specialization* derive from the Latin *spectare*—to watch, to look. In both concepts, promoters control the perceived image through the imposition of a regime of scarcity with common logistic intentions. Formal aspects such as uniformity, absolute order, and cosmic rhythm reveal the spectacle's visual character. As a public display or exhibit, the spectacle glorifies the individual, provoking the world's loss of unity. Here, the reality is pulled apart into two ends, one of which is superior to the world. This production system gives its promoters economic control, affirming the role of progress in creating short-term profits for those in power in a world where ends are nothing and development is all.

Many people nevertheless want to obliterate or ignore these facts, to erase the past and start fresh, as if earlier events had not happened. Such people seek to evoke history at their convenience. Exceptionalism thus projects a distorted illusion of an American Dream, a pervasive misrepresentation of reality that continually acclaims and glorifies an unequal, superior kind of authority.

THE TARSNEY ACT AND THE US TREASURY DEPARTMENT'S 1915 CLASSIFICATION FOR FEDERAL BUILDINGS

During the Tarsney Act era, a standardization for the design and construction of US federal architecture, both inland and abroad, became indispensable. Although this classification remained active during preceding years for cost estimates, not until 1915 did Treasury secretary William Gibbs McAdoo issue it as part of an official written statement intended "to provide a rational system of uniformity and business economy in designing and constructing public buildings, so that buildings suitable to the public needs may be built without waste of Government money."[1] The policy established four kinds of construction:

Class A

Definition: Buildings that include a post office of the first class with annual receipts of $800,000 or over; the site forming part of a city development plan or situated on an important thoroughfare of a great city; improvements on adjoining property reaching the higher valuation of the metropolitan real estate.

Character of building: Marble or granite facing; fireproof throughout; metal frames, sashes, and doors; interior finish to include the finer grades of marble, ornamental bronze work, mahogany, etc. Public spaces to have monumental treatment, mural decorations; special interior lighting fixtures.

Class B

Definition: Buildings that include a post office of the first class with receipts from $60,000 to $800,000; valuation of adjoining property somewhat below the higher valuation of the metropolitan real estate.

Character of building: Limestone or sandstone facing; fireproof throughout; exterior frames and sash metal; interior frames, sash, and doors wood; interior finish to exclude the more expensive woods and marbles; ornamental metal to be used only where iron is suitable. Restricted ornament in public spaces.

Class C

Definition: Buildings that include a post office of the second class with receipts of $15,000 or over, and of the first class to $60,000 receipts; valuation of surrounding property that of a second-class city.

Character of building: Brick facing with stone or terracotta trimmings; fireproof floors; non-fireproof roof; frames, sashes, and doors wood; interior finish to exclude the more expensive woods and marbles; the latter used only where sanitary conditions demand; public spaces restricted to very simple forms of ornament.

Class D

Definition: Buildings that include a post office having annual receipts of less than $15,000; real estate values identifying only a limited investment for improvements.

Character of building: Brick facing, little stone or terracotta used; only first floor fireproof; stock sash, frames, doors, etc., where advisable; ordinary class of building, such as any businessman would consider a reasonable investment in a small town.

APPENDIX 2

BRIEF CHRONOLOGY

1823	Secretary of State John Quincy Adams issues the Monroe Doctrine
1851	The Great Exhibition, Hyde Park, London
1861–65	US Civil War
1871	Great Fire, Chicago
1872	John Gast paints *American Progress*
1893	Congress passes the Tarsney Act
1893	Charles Follen McKim founds the American Academy in Rome
1893	World's Columbian Exposition, Chicago
1893	Katharine Lee Bates writes the first draft of "America the Beautiful"
1898	Spanish-American War
1902	Release of the *Report of the Senate Park Commission* (the McMillan Plan)
1904	St. Louis World's Fair (Louisiana Purchase Exposition)
1905	Opening of the US Courthouse and Post Office (now the Birch Bayh Federal Building and US Courthouse), Indianapolis

1905	Opening of the Frank E. Moss US Courthouse, Salt Lake City
1906	Earthquake and fire, San Francisco
1906	President Theodore Roosevelt visits the Panama Canal
1907	Opening of the Alexander Hamilton US Custom House, New York City
1910	Opening of the US Department of Agriculture Administration Building, Washington, DC
1910	Formation of the US Commission of Fine Arts
1913	Congress repeals the Tarsney Act
1914	Opening of the Panama Canal and the Panama Canal Administration Building, Balboa
1914–18	World War I
1915	Opening of the US Courthouse and Post Office (now the US Bankruptcy Court), Dayton, Ohio
1915	Panama-Pacific International Exposition, San Francisco
1915–17	Panama-California International Exposition, San Diego
1929	Opening of Capitolio, Havana, Cuba
1929	Opening of Capitolio, San Juan, Puerto Rico

GLOSSARY OF ARCHITECTURAL TERMS

arcade: A line of counterthrusting arches raised on columns or piers (Harris, *Illustrated Dictionary of Historic Architecture*, 26).

architrave: In the classical orders, the lowest member of the **entablature**; the beam that spans from column to column, resting directly upon their capitals. The ornamental moldings around the faces of the jambs and lintel of a doorway or other opening (Harris, *Dictionary of Architecture and Construction*, 29).

baluster: One of a number of short vertical members, often circular in section, used to support a stair handrail or a coping (*Historic Architecture*, 42).

Baroque: A European style of architecture and decoration that developed in the seventeenth century in Italy from late Renaissance and Mannerist forms. It is characterized by interpenetration of oval spaces, curved surfaces, and conspicuous use of decoration, sculpture, and color. Its late phase is called Rococo (*Historic Architecture*, 46).

Baroque Churrigueresque: The lavish ornamented style of the early eighteenth century, named after the Spanish architect José Benito de Churriguera (1665–1725) (*Historic Architecture*, 115).

base: The lowest (and often widest) visible part of a building, often distinctively treated. A base is distinguished from a foundation or footing in being visible rather than buried. A low, thickened section of a wall; a wall base. The lower part of a column or pier, wider than the shaft, and resting on a plinth or pedestal (*Architecture and Construction*, 48).

bas-relief: A carving, embossing, or casting moderately protruded from the background plane; **low relief** (*Historic Architecture*, 51).

Beaux-Arts: The "fine arts" (French); from the École des Beaux-Arts, Paris, and the widely imitated conventional type of art and architecture advocated there (etymonline.com).

capital: The topmost member, usually decorated, of a column, **pilaster**, or the like; may be topped by an **architrave** or an **arcade** (*Architecture and Construction*, 89).

Classical Revival: An architectural movement based on the use of pure Roman and Greek forms, mainly in England and the USA in the early nineteenth century, but in a wider sense in all of Western Europe in reaction to Rococo and Baroque design. One can distinguish between Greek Revival and Roman Revival (*Historic Architecture*, 119).

classicism: In architecture, principles that emphasize the correct use not only of Roman and Greek, but also of Italian Renaissance models (*Historic Architecture*, 119).

coffers: Deeply recessed and often highly ornamented panels in a ceiling (*Architecture and Construction*, 123).

colonnade: Columns arranged at intervals and supporting an **entablature** and usually one side of a roof (*Architecture and Construction*, 125).

Corinthian/Corinthian order: The slenderest and most ornate of the three Greek orders, characterized by a bell-shaped capital with volutes and two rows of acanthus leaves, and with an elaborate **cornice** (*Historic Architecture*, 138).

cornice: The third or uppermost division of an **entablature**, resting on the **frieze** (*Historic Architecture*, 142).

cupola: A domical roof on a circular base, often set on a ridge (*Historic Architecture*, 152).

dentil: One of a band of small, square, tooth-like blocks forming part of the characteristic ornamentation of the **Ionic**, **Corinthian**, and Composite orders, and sometimes the **Doric** (*Historic Architecture*, 161).

dome: A curved roof structure spanning an area; often hemispherical in shape. Also, a vault substantially hemispherical in shape, but sometimes slightly pointed or bulbous; a ceiling of similar form (*Historic Architecture*, 166).

Doric order: The column and **entablature** developed by the Dorian Greeks, sturdy in proportion, with a simple cushion capital, a **frieze** of triglyphs and metopes, and mutules in the **cornice** (*Historic Architecture*, 172).

entablature: In classical architecture, the elaborated beam carried by the columns, horizontally divided into **architrave** (below), **frieze**, and **cornice** (above) (*Historic Architecture*, 197).

frieze: The middle horizontal member of a classical **entablature**, above the **architrave** and below the **cornice** (*Architecture and Construction*, 235).

high relief: Sculpture relief work in which the figures project more than their thickness (*Historic Architecture*, 284).

International Style: The functional architecture devoid of regional characteristics, created in Western Europe and the USA during the early twentieth century and applied throughout the world (*Historic Architecture*, 300).

Ionic order: The classical order of architecture, originated by the Ionian Greeks, characterized by its capital with large volutes, a fascinated **entablature**, continuous **frieze**, usually **dentils** in the **cornice**, and by its elegant detailing, less heavy than the **Doric**, less elaborate than the **Corinthian** (*Historic Architecture*, 302).

Italian Renaissance Revival: The eclectic form of country-house design, fashionable in England and the US in the 1840s and 1850s, characterized by low-pitched, heavily bracketed roofs, asymmetrical informal plan, square towers, and often round-arched windows (*Historic Architecture*, 307).

lantern: A windowed superstructure crowning a roof or dome; also called a lantern light (*Historic Architecture*, 325).

loggia: An arcaded or colonnaded porch or gallery attached to a larger structure (*Historic Architecture*, 332).

low relief: Same as **bas-relief** (*Historic Architecture*, 341).

Mannerism: Transitional style in architecture and the arts in the late sixteenth century, particularly in Italy, characterized in architecture by an unconventional use of classical elements (*Historic Architecture*, 345).

metope: The panel between the triglyphs in the **Doric frieze**, often carved (*Historic Architecture*, 353).

mission architecture: Church and monastery architecture of the Spanish religious orders in Mexico and California, mainly in the eighteenth century (*Historic Architecture*, 355).

Modernismo: The Spanish, particularly Catalan, version of Art Nouveau (*Historic Architecture*, 356).

modern movement: Twentieth-century architectural movement (also called modernism) that sought to sunder all stylistic and historic links with the past. The aims of modernism were radical, concerned with the suppression of all ornament, historical allusions, and styles, counterbalanced by the elevation of *Sachlichkeit* (objectivity) and the evolution of industrialized methods of build-ing. Some groups within the modern movement, such as De Stijl, advocated abstractions and purity of expression, and there were various emphases within the overall movement, but virtually all were agreed on the need for rational responses to contemporary needs using modern materials, mass-produced building components, and experimental, industrial methods of construction (encyclopedia.com).

neoclassicism: The last phase of European classicism, in the late eighteenth and nineteenth centuries, characterized by monumentality, strict use of the orders, and sparing application of ornament (*Historic Architecture*, 372).

Néo-Grec: An architectural style developed in France in the 1840s, applying Greek forms to brick and cast iron (*Historic Architecture*, 372).

Neo-Mudéjar: A type of Moorish Revival architecture practiced in the Iberian Peninsula and to a far lesser extent in Ibero-America. This architectural movement emerged as a revival of Mudéjar style. It was an architectural trend of the late nineteenth and early twentieth centuries that began in Madrid and Barcelona and quickly spread to other regions in Spain and Portugal. It used Mudéjar style elements such as the horseshoe arch, arabesque tiling, and abstract shaped brick ornamentations for the facades of modern buildings (wikipedia.org).

parti: A scheme or concept for the design of a building (*Architecture and Construction*, 590).

pediment: In classical architecture, the triangular gable end of the roof above the horizontal **cornice**, often filled with sculpture. In later work, a surface used ornamentally over doors or windows; usually triangular but may be curved (*Architecture and Construction*, 405).

peristyle: A **colonnade** surrounding either the exterior of a building or an open space, e.g., a courtyard. Also, the space so enclosed (*Historic Architecture*, 409).

pilaster: An engaged pier or pillar, often with **capital** and **base**. Also, decorative features that imitate engaged piers but are not supporting structures, as a rectangular or semicircular member used as a simulated pillar in entrances and other door openings and fireplace mantels; often contains a **base**, shaft, and **capital**; may be constructed as a projection of the wall itself (*Historic Architecture*, 423).

plateresque: "Silversmith-like," the richly decorative style of the Spanish Renaissance in the sixteenth century. Its early phase is also referred to as Isabelline architecture, after Queen Isabella (1474–1504) (*Historic Architecture*, 424).

plinth: A square or rectangular base for column, **pilaster**, or door framing (*Architecture and Construction*, 424).

portico: A porch or covered walk consisting of a roof supported by columns; a colonnaded (continuous row of columns) porch. Also, a freestanding roofed colonnade; a stoa (*Historic Architecture*, 431).

Romanesque: The style emerging in Western Europe in the early eleventh century, based on Roman and Byzantine elements, characterized by massive articulated wall structures, round arches, and powerful vaults, and lasting until the advent of Gothic architecture in the middle of the twelfth century (*Historic Architecture*, 461).

rotunda: A circular hall in a large building, especially one covered by a **cupola** (*Historic Architecture*, 471).

salle des pas-perdus: A large vestibule or hall communicating with the various offices and other rooms of a building open to the public: train station, city hall, courthouse, etc. (Wikipedia).

Spanish Baroque: Spanish Baroque is inspired by the Counter-Reformation of the Catholic church during the 1600s. Spanish Baroque architecture focused less on the building itself and more on the ornamentation around doors, windows, and altars. The interior walls are simple and plain, acting as a backdrop for the more elaborate windows and altars. After traveling from Italy in the mid-1600s, the Spanish Baroque architectural period lasted from the middle of the seventeenth century and into the middle of the eighteenth century. The characteristics of Spanish Baroque architecture are plain basic construction out of brick with the use of stone for the decoration of facades. Spanish Baroque art is known for its visual realism with fluid brush strokes and no visible outlines. The color palette is darker and has more earthy tones than its Italian counterpart (study.com).

Spanish Colonial Revival: The Spanish Colonial Revival style includes a wide range of elements influenced by Spanish colonial architecture in the United States. The style's bright stucco walls and red tile roofs have a distinctly Mediterranean flair that seems appropriate for the style's Southern California origins, but revival architecture of this sort can be found throughout the country. Examples can incorporate elements from the broad history of Spanish architecture, including Moorish, Gothic, Byzantine, and Renaissance sources (isarchitecture.com).

Spanish Renaissance Revival: Structures in this style are often asymmetrical. They may have multiple smaller sections connected by courtyards, arcades, or walkways. Often, they have stucco walls—brick or stone covered in a clay substance (study.com).

tapis vert: An unbroken expanse of lawn used as a major element of a landscape design (collinsdictionary.com).

triglyph: The characteristic ornament of the **Doric frieze**, consisting of slightly raised blocks of three vertical bands separated by V-shaped grooves. The triglyphs alternate with plain or sculptured panels called metopes (*Historic Architecture*, 551).

verde antique: A serpentinite breccia popular since ancient times as a decorative facing stone. It is a dark, dull green, white-mottled (or white-veined) serpentine, mixed with calcite, dolomite, or magnesite, which takes a high polish. The term verd antique has been documented in English texts as early as 1745 (wikipedia.org).

vestibule: An anteroom or small foyer leading into a larger space (*Historic Architecture*, 564).

Book References

Harris, Cyril M., ed. *Dictionary of Architecture and Construction*. New York: McGraw-Hill, 1975.
Harris, Cyril M., ed. *Illustrated Dictionary of Historic Architecture*. New York: Dover, 1977.

NOTES

CHAPTER 1: AMERICAN EXCEPTIONALISM: ARTISTIC AND ARCHITECTURAL PRECEDENTS

1. Turner, *Significance of the Frontier*, 3–4.
2. Go, *Patterns of Empire*, 6.
3. For exceptionalism, see Go, *Patterns of Empire*, 2. For an interpretation of an "object of desire" via an objet petit a, see Lacan, *Seminar of Jacques Lacan*, 103–5.
4. Vale, *Architecture, Power, and National Identity*, 48–49.
5. Theodore Roosevelt, speech, Chicago, April 2, 1903, in Roosevelt, *Presidential Addresses and State Papers*, 266.
6. Lee, *Architects to the Nation*, 107.
7. "Erection of Public Buildings," 56.
8. Lee, *Architects to the Nation*, 202–7.
9. Weizman, *Forensic Architecture*, 6.
10. Schopenhauer, *Essays and Aphorisms*, 155–65.
11. Bates, *America the Beautiful*.
12. Grossman, *Civic Architecture*, 35.
13. Moore, *Improvement of the Park System*.
14. Huhtamo, *Illusions in Motion*, 12.
15. Huhtamo, *Illusions in Motion*, 77.

CHAPTER 2: RELEVANT EXAMPLES OF US CIVIC BEAUX-ARTS ARCHITECTURE

1. "Birch Bayh Federal Building."
2. Wilson, *McKim, Mead & White, Architects*, 168.
3. *Puerto Rico's House of Laws*, 1.
4. García, "El Neocolonial 'a lo cubano,'" 7.
5. Checo et al., *National Palace*, 46–47.
6. Haskins, *Canal Zone Pilot*.

7. *South of Panama.*
8. Bland and Jensen, *Oh Panama!*
9. Ormsbee, "Panama Canal Treaty Transition."

CHAPTER 3: RELEVANT DESIGNERS FROM THE TARSNEY ACT ERA

1. Grossman, *Civic Architecture*, 58–59.
2. Mumford, *Brown Decades*, 83.
3. Moore, *Daniel H. Burnham*, 36.
4. Jackson, *Pioneer of Tropical Landscape Architecture*, 31.
5. Brown, *Papers Related to the Improvement*, 79–80.

AFTERWORD: GUY DEBORD (1931-1994) AND HIS EXCEPTIONALIST SPECTACLE

1. Debord, *Society of the Spectacle*, 17.

APPENDIX 1: THE TARSNEY ACT AND THE US TREASURY DEPARTMENT'S 1915 CLASSIFICATION FOR FEDERAL BUILDINGS

1. US Treasury Department, *Annual Report*, 31.

BIBLIOGRAPHY

Alofsin, Anthony. *The Struggle for Modernism: Architecture, Landscape Architecture and City Planning at Harvard*. New York: W. W. Norton, 2002.

Ameringer, Charles D. "Ohio and the Panama Canal." *Ohio History Journal* 74, no. 1 (Winter 1965): 3–12, 69–70.

"Anexos del Capitolio: Senado y Cámara de Representantes." http://www.puertadetierra .info/edificios/anexos/anexos.htm. Accessed March 5, 2023.

Annual Report of the Isthmian Canal Commission. Washington, DC: US Government Printing Office, 1911–14.

Baltrusaitis, Jurgis. *Aberrations: An Essay on the Legend of Forms*. Cambridge: MIT Press, 1989.

Baltrusaitis, Jurgis. *Anamorphic Art*. Cambridge: Chadwick-Healey, 1977.

Bataille, Georges. *Visions of Excess: Selected Writings, 1927–1939*. Minneapolis: University of Minnesota Press, 1985.

Bates, Katharine Lee. *America the Beautiful and Other Classic Poems*. South Yarra, Victoria: Leopold Classic Library, 2016.

Batey, Mavis. "The Picturesque: An Overview." *Garden History: The Picturesque* 22, no. 2 (Winter 1994): 121–32.

Baudelaire, Charles. 2012. "The Dandy." In *The Bloomsbury Anthology of Aesthetics*, ed. Joseph Tanke and Colin McQuillan. New York: Bloomsbury Academic, 2012.

Baudrillard, Jean. *Simulacra and Simulation*. Ann Arbor: University of Michigan Press, 2000.

Benjamin, Walter. *The Work of Art in the Age of Mechanical Reproduction*. Los Angeles: UCLA School of Theater, Film, and Television, 1936.

Bennitt, Mark. *History of the Louisiana Purchase Exposition: Comprising the History of the Louisiana Territory, the Story of the Louisiana Purchase and a Full Account of the Great Exposition, Embracing the Participation of the States and Nations of the World, and Other Events of the St. Louis World's Fair of 1904*. St. Louis: Universal Exposition Publishing, 1905.

Berbusse, Edward J. *The United States in Puerto Rico, 1898–1900*. Chapel Hill: University of North Carolina Press, 1966.

Bilbo, Rebecca W. "Gertrude Vanderbilt Whitney: Patron of the American Realists." Master's thesis, University of Cincinnati, 1985.

"Birch Bayh Federal Building." https://www.gsa.gov/historic-buildings/birch-bayh-federal
-building-and-us-courthouse-indianapolis.

Blackwell, Russell. *The Architects of America: How the Freemasons Designed the Republic.*
New York: Algora, 2012.

Bland, Bartholomew, and Kirsten Jensen. *Oh Panama! Jonas Lie Paints the Panama Canal.*
Yonkers, NY: Hudson River Museum, 2016.

Boime, Albert. *The Magisterial Gaze: Manifest Destiny and American Landscape, c. 1830–1865.*
Washington, DC: Smithsonian Institution Press, 1991.

Bolotin, Norman, and Christine Laing. *The World's Columbian Exposition: The Chicago
World's Fair of 1893.* Urbana: University of Illinois Press, 2002.

Brockett, Oscar, and Franklin Hildy. *History of the Theatre.* Boston: Allyn and Bacon, 2003.

Brooklyn Museum. *The American Renaissance, 1876–1917.* New York: Pantheon, 1979.

Brown, Glenn, ed. *Papers Related to the Improvement of the City of Washington, District of
Columbia.* Washington, DC: US Government Printing Office, 1901.

Bruno, Lee. *Panorama: Tales from San Francisco's 1915 Pan-Pacific International Exposition.*
Petaluma, CA: Cameron, 2014.

"Canal Office Building." *Canal Record,* December 30, 1914.

Casey, Edward S. *Representing Place: Landscape Painting and Maps.* Minneapolis: University
of Minnesota Press, 2002.

Castillero, Ernesto. *Historia de Panamá.* Panama City: Ministerio de Educación, 1989.

Checo, José Chez, Emilio José Brea García, Denise Morales, Guillermina Nadal Zayas,
and Limary Gutiérrez. *The National Palace: 50 Years of History and Architecture.* Santo
Domingo, DR: Administrative Secretariat of the Presidency, 2008.

Cody, Jeffrey W. *Exporting American Architecture, 1870–2000.* London: Routledge, 2003.

Colon to Panama Canal Picture. American Mutoscope and Biograph, 1907.

Costello, Diarmuid. "Museum as Work in the Age of Technological Display: Reading
Heidegger through Tate Modern." In *Art and Thought: New Interventions in Art History,*
ed. Dana Arnold and Margaret Iversen. Malden, MA: Blackwell, 2003.

Curtis, Nathaniel C. *Secrets of Architectural Composition.* New York: Dover, 2013.

Dalrymple, Dana. "Agriculture, Architects, and the Mall, 1901–1905: The Plan Is Tested." In
Designing the Nation's Capital: The 1901 Plan for Washington, DC, ed. Sue Kohler and
Pamela Scott. Washington, DC: US Commission of Fine Arts, 2006.

"Daniel H. Burnham: Plans for the Philippines." https://burnhampi.wordpress.com/.
Accessed March 5, 2023.

Debord, Guy. *The Society of the Spectacle.* New York: Zone, 1995.

Drexler, Arthur, ed. *The Architecture of the École des Beaux-Arts.* New York: Museum of
Modern Art, 1977.

"Erection of Public Buildings." *Architecture and Building* 18, no. 5 (February 4, 1893): 56.

Erroz, Francisco J. *Arquitectos del siglo XX en Panamá: Un siglo de arquitectura, 1903–2003.*
Panamá: Imprenta Universitaria, 2004.

Fernandez, Ronald, Serafín Méndez, and Gail Cueto. 1998. *Puerto Rico Past and Present: An
Encyclopedia.* Westport, CT: Greenwood, 1998

Forestier, J. C. N. *Gardens: A Note-book of Plans and Sketches.* New York: Scribner's, 1928.

Foster, Hal, ed. *Vision and Visuality.* Seattle: Bay, 1988.

Friedman, B. H. *Gertrude Vanderbilt Whitney.* New York: Doubleday, 1978.

García, Alicia. "El Neocolonial 'a lo cubano' de Govantes y Cabarrocas: El Pabellón Cuba de
Sevilla y Xanadú de Varadero." *Arquitectura y Urbanismo* 32, no. 1 (2011): 7–16.

Gelernter, Mark. *A History of American Architecture: Buildings in Their Cultural and Technological Context*. Hanover, NH: University Press of New England, 1999.

Gilbert, Helen, and Joanne Tompkins. *Post-Colonial Drama: Theory, Practice, Politics*. London: Routledge, 1996.

Gill, Brendan. *Many Masks: A Life of Frank Lloyd Wright*. Boston: Da Capo, 1998.

Go, Julian. *Patterns of Empire: The British and American Empires, 1688 to the Present*. New York: Cambridge University Press, 2011.

Goodwin, Doris Kearns. *The Bully Pulpit: Theodore Roosevelt, William Howard Taft, and the Golden Age of Journalism*. New York: Simon and Schuster, 2013.

Greenberg, Allan, and Michael George. *The Architecture of McKim, Mead, and White, 1879–1915*. Lanham, MD: Architectural Book Publishing, 2013.

Grossman, Elizabeth Greenwell. *The Civic Architecture of Paul Cret*. Cambridge: Cambridge University Press, 1996.

Grossman, Elizabeth Greenwell. "Paul Philippe Cret: Rationalism and Imagery in American Architecture." Master's thesis, Brown University, 1980.

Guía de el Capitolio. Havana: Com-Relieve and Editorial Escudo de Oro, 1998.

Gutiérrez, Samuel. *Arquitectura de la Época del Canal: 1880–1914 y sus paralelos norteamericanos, franceses y caribeños*. Panama City: EUPAN, 1984.

Gutiérrez, Samuel. *Arquitectura panameña: Descripción e historia*. Panamá: Editorial Litográfica, 1967.

Harbeson, John. *The Study of Architectural Design: With Special Reference to the Program of the Beaux-Arts Institute of Design*. New York: Norton, 2008.

Harris, Cyril M., ed. *Dictionary of Architecture and Construction*. New York: McGraw-Hill, 1975.

Harris, Cyril M., ed. *Illustrated Dictionary of Historic Architecture*. New York: Dover, 1977.

Haskins, William C. *Canal Zone Pilot: Guide to the Republic of Panama*. Panama City: Star & Herald, 1908.

Heidegger, Martin. *Being and Time*. San Francisco: Harper and Row, 1962.

Heidegger, Martin. *Poetry, Language, Thought*. San Francisco: Harper and Row, 1971.

Hollier, Denis. *Against Architecture: The Writings of Georges Bataille*. Cambridge: MIT Press, 1989.

Howard, Ebenezer. *Garden Cities of To-morrow*. 1902. Lexington, KY, 2013.

Huhtamo, Erkki. *Illusions in Motion: Media Archaeology of the Moving Panorama and Related Spectacles*. Cambridge: MIT Press, 2013.

Jackson, Faith Reyher. *Pioneer of Tropical Landscape Architecture: William Lyman Phillips in Florida*. Gainesville: University Press of Florida, 1997.

Jones, Robert. 2017. *Branding: A Very Short Introduction*. Oxford, UK: Oxford University Press.

Jordy, William. *American Buildings and Their Architects: Progressive and Academic Ideals at the Turn of the Twentieth Century*. New York: Oxford University Press, 1972.

Kavaratzis, Mihalis, Gary Warnaby, and Gregory J. Ashworth. *Rethinking Place Branding: Comprehensive Brand Development for Cities and Regions*. Cham, Switzerland: Springer International, 2015.

Kidney, Walter C. *The Architecture of Choice: Eclecticism in America, 1880–1930*. New York: Braziller, 1974.

Klingmann, Anna. *Brandscapes: Architecture in the Experience Economy*. Cambridge: MIT Press, 2007.

Kohler, Sue. *The Commission of Fine Arts: A Brief History*. Washington, DC: Commission of
    Fine Arts, 1991.
Lacan, Jacques. *The Seminar of Jacques Lacan: The Four Fundamental Concepts of Psychoanalysis*.
    Book 9. New York: Norton, 1978.
Laugier Marc-Antoine. *Essay on Architecture*. 1753. Los Angeles: Hennessey and Ingalls, 1977.
Lee, Antoinette. *Architects to the Nation: The Rise and Decline of the Supervising Architect's
    Office*. New York: Oxford University Press, 2000.
Levine, Neil. "The Romantic Idea of Architectural Legibility: Henri Labrouste and the Néo-
    Grec." In *The Architecture of the École des Beaux-Arts*, ed. Arthur Drexler. New York:
    Museum of Modern Art; Cambridge: MIT Press, 1977.
Longstreth, Richard, ed. *The Mall in Washington, 1791–1991*. New Haven: Yale University
    Press, 2002.
Loos, Adolph. *Ornament and Crime: Selected Essays*. Riverside, CA: Ariadne, 1998.
Lowenstein, M. J., comp. *Official Guide to the Louisiana Purchase Exposition at the City of St.
    Louis, State of Missouri, April 30th to December 1st, 1904*. St. Louis: Louisiana Purchase
    Exposition, 1904.
Luebke, Thomas, ed. 2013. *Civic Art: A Centennial History of the U.S. Commission of Fine
    Arts*. Washington, DC: US Commission of Fine Arts.
Mackay, Robert, Anthony Baker, and Carol Traynor, eds. *Long Island Country Houses and
    Their Architects, 1860–1940*. New York: Norton, 1997.
MacNulty, W. Kirk. *Freemasonry: Symbols, Secrets, Significance*. London: Thames and
    Hudson, 2006.
Markus, Thomas. *Buildings and Power: Freedom and Control in the Origin of Modern
    Building Types*. London: Routledge, 1993.
Martín Z., María, and Rodríguez F. Eduardo. *La Habana: Guía de arquitectura*. Seville, Spain:
    Junta de Andalucía, 1998.
Mignucci, Andrés. *[Con]Textos: El Parque Muñoz Rivera y el Tribunal Supremo de Puerto
    Rico*. San Juan, PR: La Rama Judicial, 2012.
Minutes of Meetings of the Isthmian Canal Commission. Washington, DC: US Government
    Printing Office, 1911–14.
Moore, Charles. *Daniel H. Burnham, Architect, Planner of Cities*. Boston: Houghton Mifflin, 1921.
Moore, Charles. *The Improvement of the Park System of the District of Columbia*. Washington,
    DC: US Government Printing Office, 1902.
Moore, Charles. *The Life and Times of Charles McKim*. New York: Da Capo, 1970.
Mumford, Lewis. *The Brown Decades: A Study in the Arts in America, 1865–1895*. New York:
    Dover, 1955.
O'Gorman, James F. *H. H. Richardson: Architectural Forms for an American Society*. Chicago:
    University of Chicago Press, 1987.
O'Gorman, James F. *Three American Architects: Richardson, Sullivan, and Wright, 1865–1915*.
    Chicago: University of Chicago Press, 1991.
Old Market Place, Panama. Edison, 1907.
Oleksijczuk, Denise B. *The First Panoramas: Visions of British Imperialism*. Minneapolis:
    University of Minnesota Press, 2011.
Ormsbee, William H., Jr. "Panama Canal Treaty Transition—Military: Summary of Military
    Property Transfers and Military Forces Drawdown." 2008. http://william_h_ormsbee
    .tripod.com/treaty_trans_summ_mil_p01.htm.

O'Sullivan, John. "Annexation." *United States Magazine and Democratic Review* 17, no. 1 (July–August 1845): 5–10.

The Panama Canal. Hagy Features, 1914.

Peralta, Bertalicia. *Invasión U.S.A., 1989: Crónicas de una memoria.* Panama City: Universidad de Panamá, Imprenta Universitaria, 1990.

Pérez-Gómez, Alberto, and Louise Pelletier, eds. *Anamorphosis: An Annotated Bibliography: With Special Reference to Architectural Representation.* Montreal: McGill Queens University Press, 1996.

Puerto Rico's House of Laws. San Juan, PR: House of Representatives, Commonwealth of Puerto Rico, 1966.

Rebori, A. N. "The Work of William E. Parsons in the Philippine Islands, Part I." *Architectural Record* 41 (1917): 305–24.

Rebori, A. N. "The Work of William E. Parsons in the Philippine Islands, Part II." *Architectural Record* 41 (1917): 423–34.

Reps, John W. *The Making of Urban America: A History of City Planning in the United States.* Princeton: Princeton University Press, 1965.

Roosevelt, Theodore. *Presidential Addresses and State Papers.* Pt. 1. Vol. 13 of *The Works of Theodore Roosevelt.* Executive ed. New York: Co-operative Publication Society, n.d.

Roth, Leland. *American Architecture: A History.* Boulder, CO: Westview, 2001.

Roth, Leland. *Shingle Styles: Innovation and Tradition in American Architecture, 1874 to 1982.* New York: Abrams, 1999.

Ruskin, John. *Seven Lamps of Architecture.* 1849. Breinigsville, PA: General Books, 2009.

Said, Edward. *Culture and Imperialism.* New York: Vintage, 1993.

Said, Edward. *Orientalism.* New York: Vintage, 1994.

Saint, Andrew. *Architect and Engineer: A Study in Sibling Rivalry.* New Haven: Yale University Press, 2007.

Santalla G., Ernesto. "The Capitol of Puerto Rico, San Juan, Puerto Rico." Master's thesis, Cornell University, 1984.

Santovenia, Emeterio. *República de Cuba. Capitolio.* Havana: Fernández, 1933.

Schopenhauer, Arthur. *Essays and Aphorisms.* London: Penguin, 1970.

Seal, Bobby. "Baudelaire, Benjamin and the Birth of the Flâneur." *Psychogeographic Review,* November 14, 2013. https://psychogeographicreview.com/baudelaire-benjamin-and -the-birth-of-the-flaneur/.

Silko, Leslie Marmon. *Yellow Woman and a Beauty of the Spirit: Essays on Native American Life Today.* New York: Simon and Schuster, 1997.

Sklar, Barry, and Virginia Hagen, comps. *Inter-American Relations: A Collection of Documents, Legislation, Descriptions of Inter-American Organizations, and Other Material Pertaining to Inter-American Affairs.* Washington, DC: US Government Printing Office, 1972.

South of Panama. Chesterfield Motion Picture Corp., 1928.

Tejeira D., Eduardo. *Roots of Modern Latin American Architecture: The Hispano-Caribbean Region from the Late 19th Century to the Recent Past.* Heidelberg: Deutscher Akademischer Austauschdienst, 1987.

Tuchman, Barbara W. *The Guns of August: The Proud Tower.* New York: Library of America, 2012.

Turner, Frederick Jackson. *The Significance of the Frontier in American History.* 1894, reprinted by Martino Fine Books, 2014.

Turpin, John K., and W. Barry Thomson. *New Jersey Country Houses: The Somerset Hills.* 2 vols. Far Hills, NJ: Mountain Colony, 2004–5.

Upton, Dell. *Architecture in the United States.* Oxford: Oxford University Press, 1998.

US Senate. *Panama Canal: Message from the President of the United States, Transmitting a Report by the Commission of Fine Arts in Relation to the Artistic Structure of the Panama Canal.* Washington, DC: US Government Printing Office, 1913.

US Treasury Department. *Annual Report on the Finances, 1915.* Washington, DC: US Government Printing Office, 1915.

Vale, Lawrence. *Architecture, Power, and National Identity.* London: Routledge, 2008.

Viollet-le-Duc, Eugène. *Dictionnaire raisonné de l'architecture française du XIe au XVIe siècle.* Paris: Bance, 1858–68.

Vitruvius Pollio. *Ten Books on Architecture.* New York: Cambridge University Press, 1999.

Vivoni F., Enrique. *Pedro Adolfo de Castro y Besosa: Architect of Dreams.* San Juan, PR: Archivo de Arquitectura y Construcción de la Universidad de Puerto Rico, 1999.

Wardle, Marian, and Sarah E. Boehme, eds. *Branding the American West: Paintings and Films, 1900–1950.* Norman: University of Oklahoma Press, 2016.

Weizman, Eyal. *Forensic Architecture: Notes from Fields and Forums.* Ostfildern, Germany: Hatje Cantz, 2012.

Wilson, Richard Guy. "Imperial American Identity at the Panama Canal." *Modulus 1980–81: The University of Virginia School of Architecture Review* (1981): 22–29.

Wilson, Richard Guy. *McKim, Mead & White, Architects.* New York: Rizzoli, 1983.

Wright, Gwendolyn. *The Politics of Design in French Colonial Urbanism.* Chicago: University of Chicago Press, 1991.

Wyllie, Romy. *Bertram Goodhue: His Life and Residential Architecture.* New York: Norton, 2007.

Yegül, Fikret K. *Gentlemen of Instinct and Breeding: Architecture at the American Academy in Rome, 1894–1940.* New York: Oxford University Press, 1991.

INDEX

ABOUT THE AUTHOR

Photo courtesy of the author

Maria Eugenia Achurra G. is a Fulbright Scholar who holds a PhD from the School of Architecture and Interior Design at the University of Cincinnati as well as a bachelor's in architecture from the Faculty of Architecture at the University of Panama. She is currently an architect at the US Army Corps of Engineers, Huntington (West Virginia) District.

www.ingramcontent.com/pod-product-compliance
Lightning Source LLC
Chambersburg PA
CBHW052011270326
41929CB00015B/2881